The Vitality of Senior Faculty

Snow on the Roof—Fire in the Furnace

by Carole J. Bland and William H. Bergquist
—with a special contribution by Joseph Axelrod

ASHE-ERIC Higher Education Report Volume 25, Number 7

Prepared by

ERIC Clearinghouse on Higher Education
The George Washington University
URL: www.gwu.edu/~eriche

In cooperation with

Association for the Study
of Higher Education
URL: http://www.tiger.coe.missouri.edu/~ashe

Published by

Graduate School of Education and Human Development
The George Washington University
URL: www.gwu.edu

Jonathan D. Fife, Series Editor

#38250926

Cite as

Bland, Carole J., and William H. Bergquist. 1997. *The Vitality of Senior Faculty Members: Snow on the Roof—Fire in the Furnace*. ASHE-ERIC Higher Education Report Volume 25, No. 7. Washington, D.C.: The George Washington University, Graduate School of Education and Human Development.

Library of Congress Catalog Card Number 97-75336
ISSN 0884-0040
ISBN 1-878380-79-6

Managing Editor: Lynne J. Scott
Manuscript Editor: Barbara Fishel/Editech
Cover Design by Michael David Brown, Inc., The Red Door Gallery, Rockport, ME

The ERIC Clearinghouse on Higher Education invites individuals to submit proposals for writing monographs for the *ASHE-ERIC Higher Education Report* series. Proposals must include:
1. A detailed manuscript proposal of not more than five pages.
2. A chapter-by-chapter outline.
3. A 75-word summary to be used by several review committees for the initial screening and rating of each proposal.
4. A vita and a writing sample.

ERIC Clearinghouse on Higher Education
Graduate School of Education and Human Development
The George Washington University
One Dupont Circle, Suite 630
Washington, DC 20036-1183

> *The mission of the ERIC system is to improve American education by increasing and facilitating the use of educational research and information on practice in the activities of learning, teaching, educational decision making, and research, wherever and whenever these activities take place.*

This publication was prepared partially with funding from the Office of Educational Research and Improvement, U.S. Department of Education, under contract no. ED RR-93-002008. The opinions expressed in this report do not necessarily reflect the positions or policies of OERI or the Department.

EXECUTIVE SUMMARY

By the year 2000, 50 percent of full-time faculty will be over 55, and 68 percent will be over 50. Just when many universities and colleges in America are making major shifts in their missions and their organizational structures, faculty members who are expected to implement these bold new visions will be out signing up for their senior citizen discount cards. Is it any cause for alarm?

Who Are Senior Faculty and What Role Will They Play in Meeting This Challenge?

Institutional vitality in the next century is in the hands of senior faculty members in their 50s and beyond, in the "late-middle" stage of their careers. As young and idealistic faculty in the late 1960s and early 1970s, they overwhelmed the established professoriat in both numbers and enthusiasm at a time when there never before had been such an abundance of financial resources, student enrollments, and public support.

Today, they once again have the opportunity to provide leadership in transforming American higher education. But now they and the existing conditions are vastly different.

Are Senior Faculty Vital and Productive?

On average, research productivity drops off with age, although many senior faculty remain highly productive. Further, what they produce is at least comparable in quality to that produced by younger faculty. The conclusion that age causes a decline in quantity is not supported. Rather, increased responsibilities and a shift in focus on high quality rather than quantity are likely causes.

Senior faculty commit about the same amount of time to teaching as younger faculty and have similar responsibilities for advising students. Studies on the association of age and teaching effectiveness are mixed, but no studies have found a large negative relationship.

What Are the Distinctive Assets and Needs of Senior Faculty?

Most senior faculty are confident in their teaching and research skills, and they possess a deep sense of commitment to their institutions, highly inculcated values, a vital network of professional colleagues, knowledge of the academic enterprise, and an ability to manage multiple, simultaneous projects. They value alternative viewpoints and collaboration and feel quite "generative," wishing to teach and support the next generation of faculty and their institutions. They can now perceive their careers in new ways, and they often desire expanded and diversified roles in their institutions.

In contrast, a small minority of senior faculty feel "stuck." Their career plans or personal goals have not been fulfilled, and as a result they are inclined to be unsupportive of the institution and to view younger colleagues as rivals or painful reminders of their own unfulfilled dreams.

What Factors Ensure Vital Senior Faculty?

Intrinsic factors that influence a faculty member's vitality and productivity include socialization, subject knowledge and skills, past mentors, work habits, adult career development, a vital network of colleagues, simultaneous projects under way at the same time, sufficient work time, orientation, autonomy, commitment, and morale. Studies find that extrinsic factors also influence senior faculty members' productivity and vitality. Institutions can enhance faculty members' productivity by establishing clear, coordinated goals and emphasizing core faculty functions (research and teaching), a supportive academic culture, a positive group climate, participative governance, decentralized organization, frequent communication, sufficient and accessible resources, a critical mass of faculty who have been together for a while and bring different perspectives, adequate and fair salaries and other rewards, targeted recruitment and selection, actively providing opportunities for growth, and seasoned, participative academic leadership.

How Can the Vitality of Senior Faculty Be Maintained?

In many institutions, it appears that these essential features of vitality for senior faculty (in fact for all faculty) are weakened. How do we counter this trend? To maintain the productivity of older faculty members (in fact of all faculty), a systems approach is required that addresses individual vitality features, institutional vitality features, and the essential link between them.

Institutions frequently offer a hodgepodge of faculty and organizational development strategies that are not clearly aimed at particular vitality features. Such efforts have a much smaller impact than would a similar number of efforts guided by an overall plan. An alternative to this hodgepodge is a *comprehensive* approach to individual and organizational productivity that provides a rational foundation for selecting a combination of development activities that together will have a larger impact.

This comprehensive approach begins with the understanding that the purpose of a faculty and organizational development program is quite simple: to facilitate faculty members' commitment to and ability to achieve their own career goals and their institution's goals by continually assisting and developing faculty members in areas related to their and the institution's goals, and by continually improving the organizational features that facilitate quality work. These features include, for example, mechanisms that coordinate individual goals and organizational goals, equitable personnel policies, opportunities for development, and a supportive climate. Institutional features that are especially critical for senior faculty appear to be opportunities to grow, being appreciated by the leaders of the institution, collegiality, and a commitment on the part of the leaders of the institution to academic values and the founding mission of the college or university.

Ultimately to facilitate continuous individual and collective productivity, a university or college should aim for a comprehensive development program that addresses all faculty at all ages and career stages and that continually assesses and modifies its organizational structure and processes. Realistically, most organizations must choose a few strategies from a comprehensive approach on which to focus the majority of their development strategies at any given time. Having a comprehensive approach in mind, however, allows one to best select where to focus attention.

It is puzzling why so few institutions invest significantly, either intellectually or financially, to ensure senior faculty members' competence and to make the setting more conducive for their productivity. One reason for this inaction may be the previous lack of a clear profile of the features that affect senior faculty members' productivity. Without this information, leaders are unclear about where to invest resources and thus are reticent to do so.

Senior faculty are perhaps most interesting and capable at this point in their lives. Their fires still burn! Whether they are still vital—or can once again be vital—largely depends on the organization. The "graying" faculty who have effectively served our collegiate institutions for many years certainly deserve this attention. More pragmatically, they require this attention if colleges and universities are to be successfully redesigned to meet the challenges and needs of the 21st century.

CONTENTS

FOREWORD

True or false—older faculty are overpaid and unproductive compared with younger faculty. Answer—almost true and almost false. Our higher education institutions have enough highly productive older faculty to make this statement false, but there are also enough stories about unproductive senior faculty to make it very believable to state legislators and senior administrators. Whether the statement is true or false, all higher education institutions in this country must become aware that, for the next 10 years, a significant percentage of faculty will be tenured and between the ages of 55 and 70 and that an institution's ability to achieve its educational mission depends upon the productivity of this portion of their faculty.

Institutions need to examine their organizational culture, values, and procedures to create a climate that will foster high productivity for senior (as well as junior) faculty. In general, several conditions within the academic culture subtly but effectively discourage senior faculty from being productive: (1) academic leadership through benign neglect; (2) intellectual and professional nonrenewal; and (3) ignorance or different intellectual stages of productivity.

Benign neglect. After they reach the position of full professor with tenure, faculty are often perceived as untouchable and uncontrollable. Administrators, especially department chairs and deans, are inclined to give their attention to the issues they have direct control over, using their energies to fight daily administrative fires and allowing senior faculty to function without a sense of purpose or appreciation. In this atmosphere of benign neglect, many senior faculty fall into a comfortable but less productive pattern until they retire.

A lack of professional development. As a percentage of total faculty salaries, higher education institutions spend an embarrassingly small amount on professional development for their faculty compared with any other industry in this country. Funds that are allocated usually go to faculty who actively seek them and actively participate at professional association meetings. Junior faculty, who must participate at such meetings to climb the professional ladder for promotion most often actively seek funds. Senior faculty, whose careers are no longer significantly influenced by professional development, often are willing to allow their junior colleagues to use the funds for professional development.

Nonrecognition of the stages of productivity. Higher education institutions usually measure productivity the same for junior and senior faculty. As faculty mature, however, they tend to move from more quickly produced journal articles to longer-term research projects whose ultimate goal is to establish new principles or theories. Academic leaders need to understand the different intellectual stages of faculty and the support systems that will help faculty be productive at each stage.

This report, by Carole J. Bland, professor of family practice and community health in the University of Minnesota Medical School, and William H. Bergquist, independent consultant for more than 500 colleges and universities throughout North America, creatively examines the research and literature addressing the issue of senior faculty members' productivity. Through the use of a case study developed by Joseph Axelrod, the authors trace the changing productivity of a fictional faculty member, Stephen Abbott. They then examine the literature that helps to explain how faculty vitality is affected and how it might change as faculty mature. The authors conclude their report with specific recommendations for how to influence faculty and institutional vitality, addressing specific institutional policies on linking faculty evaluation and development, career alternatives, and early retirement.

Academic leaders must understand their responsibility to ensure that institutions' processes and systems support and nurture the productivity of senior faculty. Part of this task is to make sure that senior faculty have a sense of being appreciated and find purpose in their work. But academic leaders also need to ensure that the definitions of and expectations for productivity are clear. Institutions must see that their policies concerning funds for professional development, use of graduate assistants, and the like are designed to support the productivity of senior faculty. It is the purpose of this report to form the basis for conversations within the institution that will help make it more nurturing and supportive for senior faculty and in turn increase their productivity.

Jonathan D. Fife
Series Editor,
Professor of Higher Education Administration, and
Director, ERIC Clearinghouse on Higher Education

ACKNOWLEDGMENTS

This publication began a few years ago when we discovered we were both interested in, and writing about, senior faculty. We had known of each other's writings and occasionally served on national review teams together over the past 20 years, but we had never worked as partners on a project. Then in 1993, Bill and his colleagues published a book entitled *In Our Fifties: Voices of Men and Women Reinventing Their Lives.* After reading it, Carole called Bill to say how much she enjoyed the book and to share with him that it reinforced much of what she was reporting in an article on which she was working about the productivity of senior faculty. This conversation ended with a decision to work together on reporting what we know about the vitality of senior faculty.

Thus, this is the first project on which we have had the pleasure of collaborating. Being in different institutions and separated by half the country (Carole lives in Minnesota, Bill in Maine for half the year and California the other half) made it an interesting and challenging project, but we were actually in the same room working on the book once, for half a day! Thank goodness for e-mail, fax machines, Federal Express, and the U.S. Postal Service. But, mostly we want to thank the staff at the University of Minnesota who supported us in the development of this book. Without their constant attention to this project, it would never have been completed. In fact, it is in recognition of their efforts that Carole is listed as first author of this monograph. Over the time we wrote the report, life continued to happen for both of us, resulting in Bill's taking the lead part of the time and Carole's taking the lead the other part. The contributions of both authors were so similar that we could not honestly identify one of us as the lead author. In our discussions about how to resolve the order of authorship, we also tried to find a way to acknowledge the significant contributions of the Minnesota staff and the institutional support. Specifically, at the Department of Family Practice and Community Health at the University of Minnesota, Barbara Behnke was the coordinator of our work, which spanned a couple of years, different word-processing systems, a continent, and occasionally several continents. She provided word processing, editing, and the final formatting of the manuscript and references. Elizabeth Greene was an essential part of this process, having provided editing, word processing, and assistance with reference management. Greg

Sax and Ross Johnson searched not only ERIC's database but others as well for relevant works and collected hundreds of articles and books for us. Libby Frost prepared figures and tables.

We are especially indebted to Joseph Axelrod for accepting our invitation to reprise his case study of Stephen Abbot— a disguised university professor on a real college campus. Abbot has been profiled twice before, but in the second section of this monograph, Axelrod reviews Abbot's early and middle academic life and provides a first look at his senior years. It is hoped that this one case study will help the reader envision how the material presented in this monograph applies to the many ways faculty members' lives can unfold, and the internal and external factors that can influence their productivity throughout their careers.

We also want to thank Jonathan Fife. Without his encouragement and patience, this monograph would never have been written. We also appreciate the thoughtful review and comments provided by the anonymous reviewers on an early version of the manuscript.

The U.S. National Center for Education Statistics graciously provided access to its National Study of Post Secondary Faculty, and the National Education Data Resource Center in Alexandria, Virginia, analyzed the data and prepared tables.

We are deeply grateful to these people, to our institutions and families that support our work, and to the numerous productive—and often senior—colleagues whose research is referenced in this monograph.

SENIOR FACULTY AND INSTITUTIONAL VITALITY

By 2000, 50 percent of full-time faculty members will be over 55 (National Center 1993; Votruba 1990), and 68 percent will be over 50. At the same time, many of the country's universities and colleges are planning to make major changes. For example, the largest higher education systems in the world, the University of California and the California State systems, will be in the middle of major face-lifts. The University of Minnesota will have revised its structure and refined its "be everything for everyone" commitment to a narrower mission.

By 2000, 50 percent of full-time faculty members will be over 55, and 68 percent will be over 50.

So just when many universities and colleges in America are making major shifts in their missions and in their organizational structures, faculty members who are expected to implement these bold new visions will be signing up for their senior citizen discount cards. Is this situation a cause for alarm? Or are we fortunate to be undertaking these major changes just when our most experienced faculty members are still on board? Are these faculty members critical assets, or are they liabilities for meeting the challenges of our new millennium? Does the fire still rage under the snowy roof? How can we best assure the continued vitality of these senior faculty members, who will be called upon to move higher education into the next century?

The Focus of This Review

The exploration of ways in which senior faculty can maintain their vitality and avoid burnout as they lead their institutions into the new century confronts two major forces operating at the present time in our society. On the one hand, we are living in an emerging postmodern world that demands change of our higher education institutions and innovation by those people who lead and teach in these institutions (Bergquist 1993b, 1995). On the other hand, many of those who now lead and teach in our colleges and universities are—or soon will be—beyond age 50, with all of the many challenges, opportunities, and problems that age brings. At the heart of the matter is the capacity of our colleges and universities to achieve and maintain professional vitality among those senior members of the faculty.

In focusing on the issue of the senior faculty's vitality—and, in turn, on the broader issue of institutional vitality—we realize that we are venturing into a complex and often ill-defined domain. "Vitality" is an elusive term that is heavily loaded with specific assumptions and values. The concept of "vitality" has been called "primitive" (Corcoran and Clark 1985), which in turn means that it is a term that holds the potential of defining (without oversimplifying) a complex and multidimensional phenomenon, integrating disparate thoughts, and leading to more specific, well-defined ideas. A concept often ascribed to John Gardner (1963), "vitality" is about continual self-renewal. It encompasses such processes as re-creation, regeneration, physical drive and durability, physical vigor, dedication to beliefs that require action, a sense of curiosity, enthusiasm, zest, caring about things, reaching out, enjoying, and risking failure (Corcoran and Clark 1985, pp. 61–62).

At an institutional level, vitality is exhibited in a clearly designed, compelling, and accepted statement of mission, in the formulation of attainable goals based on this mission, and in the enactment of programs that fulfill the mission. Institutional vitality also concerns the creation of an organizational climate or environment that empowers individuals and groups in their fulfillment of the mission and supports individuals in their own creative, productive, and energizing work life—leading them to their own continuing process of revitalization (Corcoran and Clark 1985, pp. 62–63).

In our search for concepts and strategies that can help collegiate institutions in the late 1990s to remain or achieve vitality—and, in particular, for senior faculty in those institutions to contribute to this vitality with their own revitalization—we have reviewed several bodies of literature. First, to understand the abilities and productivity of faculty members beyond 50, we looked to studies of adult and career development among faculty, faculty productivity, and institutional productivity. Second, we looked to literature on faculty development and the maintenance of professional competence for ideas on how to maintain the vitality of this important group of faculty members.

This monograph examines the internal and external factors that influence the productivity of these men and women, describes how individual and organizational features combine to make a productive faculty, and offers a comprehensive approach to maintaining the vitality of faculty members—especially those beyond 50 years of age. But first, it includes some words about who "senior faculty" are and the larger context in which senior faculty work. As background information, it provides a portrait of a senior faculty member and briefly summarizes the research on the productivity of senior faculty compared to that of other faculty members.

Who Are "Senior Faculty"?

To begin, we asked what may at first seem to be obvious: Whom exactly are we talking about in considering the "senior faculty" of our collegiate institutions? This question is not as easy to answer as one might initially assume. The phrase "senior faculty" is a complex and often confounded term potentially involving at least four variables: age, rank, status within the institution, and career achievement. The definition becomes more confusing as one delves even further into each variable:

> *The most traditional definition of senior faculty is an organizational one[,] that is, those faculty who have achieved seniority in the employing institution as defined by tenure and the rank of associate (at least) and preferably full professor. Such a definition says nothing about seniority in one's discipline, in the sense of* scholarly distinction, *which may be highly independent of organizational seniority—particularly given the current academic job market. It also says nothing about* longevity *in an academic career or even at the employing institution* (Rice and Finkelstein 1993, p. 9).

The term is at best a composite of all four variables. Those authors who have addressed the issue of senior faculty's vitality in recent years usually include all members of the faculty who are (1) full time, (2) tenured (or at the highest level of their profession), (3) working in a collegiate institution for many years (usually at least 15), and (4) more than 45 years of age. This composite definition is valid in that these four criteria often coexist, and is valuable in terms of defining a particular cluster of faculty in our collegiate institutions that is large in number and the source of both exceptional resources and potential or real problems. It is this group of faculty that is the focus of this monograph, referred to collectively as "senior faculty members."

Setting the Stage

Concern about faculty and institutional vitality is a relatively new phenomenon in American higher education.

> *During the postwar decade, when American colleges and universities were in an unprecedented stage of growth, continually adding new recruits to the faculty body and providing established faculty members with attractive opportunities for advancement, it was taken for granted that the normal circumstances of faculty life, including preparation as a graduate student, selection and promotion criteria, salary and reward incentives, and the recognition of professional success by colleagues, provided sufficient stimulation for continued growth and productive work throughout the faculty member's career. If there were exceptions, as of course was the case, these were regarded as unfortunate, but were not a matter of great concern* (Corcoran and Clark 1985, p. 57).

The world of higher education has changed dramatically in the past 20 years—as have all other sectors of our society—leading to a deeply felt concern about faculty vitality among not only those who administer and govern our colleges and universities, but also the faculty members themselves.

These concerns arise in large part from two distinct though interrelated forces: (1) greater diversification of the student population accompanied by shifting and unpredictable student needs, interests, and talents; and (2) the aging of the faculty, many of whom were appointed during the financial heyday of American higher education, in the late 1960s and early 1970s. Each of these factors impinges dramatically on the work of faculty and on the vitality of the institutions where they work. Each factor is particularly salient when consideration is given specifically to the vitality of faculty members who are now in or soon will be in their 50s.

The challenges of these two factors are further heightened by the declining—or at least vacillating—public support for collegiate education, which has led in turn to reduced or variable and unpredictable funding for teaching and research and to declining faculty status. We need vital senior faculty members at this point in the history of American higher education precisely *because* the challenges we face are great and complex. Without the wisdom of senior faculty, our institutions are likely to make many mistakes. Our colleges and universities cannot afford to relearn lessons from the past, given major challenges and limited resources.

Shifting student demographics

The students in our institutions are, in most cases, vastly different from those who populated the colleges and universities from which our senior faculty graduated in the 1950s and 1960s (Levine 1989). With regard to the challenges facing senior faculty during the 1990s, "radical changes [are] occurring in the student body in terms of race/ethnicity, age, and gender. . . . Compared to previous generations of students they have . . . very different learning styles, with very serious academic skill deficiencies, and with very wide variation in prior academic preparation" (Rice and Finkelstein 1993, p. 13). Teaching strategies and practices honed in the past (the straight lecture, for example) may no longer achieve desired results.

The new student population offers many challenges for senior faculty. They must not only, as suggested, rethink their teaching strategies, but must also reexamine their basic assumptions about the purposes of higher education and, more specifically, their assumptions about the relationships between educational quality and educational access (Bergquist 1995). Many senior faculty entered the 1990s holding the traditional assumption that quality and access are inherently incompatible and believing that some institutions have achieved high quality in part because of their strict admissions standards. From this "elitist" perspective, quality would be diminished with more open access, with "quality" being defined primarily in terms of input measures (size of library, qualifications of faculty, and so forth, as well as by qualifications of entering students). Other institutions seek to increase access but at the expense of quality. Faculty and administrators in these institutions assume a "populist" perspective, accepting the inevitability of lower educational quality for the sake of offering the benefits of higher education to as many students as possible (Bergquist 1995).

Integrating high quality and open access is essential in the 1990s. An education of high quality must expose students to diversity, given the challenges of our emerging world. And diversity is best achieved by promoting open access so that the classroom is filled with learners with different life experiences, attitudes, values, and perspectives. Conversely, educational access in the 1990s is a sham if it provides a second-rate education for those who have been traditionally underserved. A low-quality education perpetuates myths of inadequacy rather than provides the opportunity for upward social, economic, occupational, or political mobility. Put simply, quality without access is no longer (if it ever was) quality, and access without quality is not now (if it ever was) true access (Bergquist 1995).

How are senior faculty to address these challenges? If these faculty members come from an elitist perspective, how will they begin to see nontraditional learners as assets rather than as liabilities? How do faculty members from a populist perspective come to recognize the importance of setting standards for themselves and their students that are just as high as those found in more prestigious institutions, recognizing that standards can be different without being "lower"? And how do senior faculty members who have been teaching for many years come to be excited once again about the challenges that their institution faces in a changing world— in this case, embracing and integrating educational quality and access?

The challenge for any leaders of collegiate institutions thus becomes one of helping senior faculty find new ways to teach the students they are now supposed to serve and, even more important, gain a new appreciation of, and perspectives on, the rich opportunities afforded by these new students and the new concerns about integrating quality and access. The accumulated wisdom of these senior faculty members is essential to any new educational philosophy or institutional strategy that seeks to preserve what is good in the traditional ways of thinking about and achieving quality and access, and to incorporate new ideas about the essential integration of these two dimensions of educational life.

Shifting faculty demographics

Based on the National Center for Education Statistics's 1993 study of postsecondary education faculty, the predicted average age of full-time faculty in 2000 will be 48. Sixty-eight percent of the faculty, however, will be over 50 years of age, and 50 percent will be 55 or older (see table 1). The total faculty in 2000 will certainly not exactly match the group surveyed in 1993; some of this group will have retired or moved to part-time status, for example, while some new faculty will have been hired. Respondents to the survey were asked at what age they anticipate stopping work at a postsecondary institution. Twenty percent of the total full-time faculty will be at their "expected retirement age" in 2000. If these faculty do retire when anticipated or if many institutions increase the incentives to retire, the percent of faculty over age 55 in 2000 will be less then 50 percent. But the current best estimate with regard to the age of faculty in 2000 is that the large majority will be over 50 years old and that 50 percent will be 55 years of age or more.

TABLE 1

Ages and Likelihood of Retirement of All Faculty and Instructional Faculty Only by 2000

	Years of Age in 2000					
	All Faculty			**Instructional Faculty Only**[a]		
	Ave. Age	*% 50–54*	*%≥55*	*Ave. Age*	*% 50–54*	*%≥55*
Part Time	45.9	19.1	39.3	45.8	19.2	38.8
Full Time	47.8	18.2	50.0	48.0	18.2	50.6
TOTAL		16.6	45.5		18.6	45.7

	Likelihood of Retirement in 2000			
	All Faculty[b]		**Instructional Faculty Only**	
	% Not Likely to Retire	*% Likely to Retire*	*% Not Likely to Retire*	*% Likely to Retire*
Part Time	82.4	17.6	82.5	17.5
Full Time	80.5	19.5	80.1	19.9
TOTAL	81.3	18.7	81.1	18.9

[a]The variable for "instructional faculty only" was created by asking whether faculty performed any instructional duties for credit. Only those respondents answering "yes" were considered "instructional faculty."

[b]Respondents were asked when they anticipate stopping work at a postsecondary institution. This percentage indicates the proportion who will have reached this anticipated retirement age by 2000.

Source: National Center 1993. Table prepared by National Education Data Resource Center, Alexandria, Virginia.

The 1987 national survey also indicates that:

> . . . *60 percent of full-time faculty hold tenure, 22 percent are in tenure-track positions, and 9 percent are in institutions with no tenure system. In public two-year colleges . . . [where tenure often plays a less important role], 60 percent of faculty also hold tenure, but only 9 percent are in tenure-track positions, and 25 percent report that there is no system of tenure at the institution* (D. Kelly 1991, p. 3).

Many problems have been hypothesized to result from this massed cohort of senior faculty. But the reality of these problems is in question. First, the presence of many faculty at the senior end of the age spectrum means that salaries and benefits tend to cluster at the higher end of the range. Tenured full professors can be expensive and cost a college or university more money than either newly minted assistant professors or part-time, contracted faculty of any age (Renner 1991). Some financial projections indicate that the extra costs associated with fully tenured faculty in most collegiate institutions are unlikely to significantly decline until after the start of the new century and in many instances not until 2005 or even 2010 (e.g., Renner 1986). It should be noted, however, that a salary inversion has occurred in many institutions; that is, faculty have received low or no increases over the years, but institutions have had to offer competitive salaries to attract new professors. The gap between new hires and associate (and sometimes full) professors can be quite narrow. Thus, the actual savings from releasing senior faculty and hiring new ones is often small.

Second, some authors believe that because a faculty cohort is heavily weighted toward the senior and tenured end, it is much less flexible than one weighted toward the junior and untenured end (Renner 1991). They believe that there are fewer options for an institution confronted with a senior faculty and that downsizing the faculty is not much of an option for a heavily tenured collegiate institution faced with major financial difficulties (Renner 1986). But this "problem" is not so much a result of a large cohort of senior faculty as it is of narrowly identifying layoffs as the only way to save money. If one thinks more broadly about solving financial problems—for example, through retraining faculty for other roles or reassigning faculty to other income-generating activities or reallocating "faculty" dollars recovered through natural attrition—then the inability to lay off faculty is not an intractable barrier to an institution's financial stability.

In some areas of specialization, such as the sciences and technology, some authors suggest that the predominance of senior faculty creates a problem with regard to currency. As shown later, however, the research on faculty obsolescence does not support this conclusion either.

Finally, some writers suggest that senior faculty are no longer satisfied with or excited about their work or their academic careers. They are "burned out," "stuck," or simply stagnant, awaiting their next paycheck over the short term and retirement over the longer term. Again, as shown later, most senior faculty in reality do not match this profile. It is true, however, that the challenges facing senior faculty, as well as their junior colleagues, are likely to increase. Student enrollments are expected to increase, with little increase in public financial support for higher education until at least the first part of the next decade.

Moreover, when many senior faculty retire, an additional crisis will arise. Some authors suggest that our graduate schools are not producing a sufficient number of graduates to fill the slots that will be opened by the massive retirement of many faculty members. Either the quality will diminish with the hiring of new faculty who are not qualified for the position, or senior faculty will be asked to stay on while the search continues for the nonexistent young faculty member (Bowen and Schuster 1986). Even when qualified faculty members are found, they will be entering institutions whose traditions and knowledge are depleted, given that many of the senior faculty members will be retiring at the same time and taking with them years of legacy and institutional wisdom. They will, however, leave a host of institutional problems produced by years of underfunded education and deferred maintenance of buildings and grounds. They will leave behind major decisions regarding the purchase and updating of educational technology and the identification of critical changes that must be made in American higher education if it is to remain a vital force in the new millennium. We may have to retain many of our senior faculty members and ensure that they remain vital if we are to face these problems and decisions successfully.

Conclusions

The central question thus becomes, What do these shifting faculty demographics suggest about the vitality of senior faculty? First, these faculty are generally tenured in the institution where they teach. If they are not tenured, then they probably have experienced major barriers to their advancement or have been unsuccessful in meeting their primarily institutional obligations. Those who have not achieved tenure offer a special case, to which we will occasionally refer when discussing the revitalization of senior faculty who are disillusioned or "stuck." Most faculty, however, who will play a major role in leading their institutions into the next century are tenured and, as a result, "have achieved relative security and permanence both in their chosen career and in their institutional position" (Rice and Finkelstein 1993, p. 12). While some colleges and universities threaten to lay off or have already laid off senior faculty, these cases are rare and are inevitably highly controversial and hotly contested. Thus, for many senior faculty, job security is much less of a fear than for almost any profession or vocation in our society.

Second, senior faculty members have no place to go with regard to career advancement. Collegiate institutions are relatively flat, with no career development steps after one reaches the status of full professor, unless one wants to move into administration or outside the academic world. Thus, senior faculty have "typically plateaued organizationally in terms of their intrainstitutional mobility" (Rice and Finkelstein 1993, p. 12). In many fields, especially in corporate life, career plateaus are often a sign of being "stuck" and a cause for psychological withdrawal from work in search of other sources of gratification (Baldwin 1990; Kanter 1977). Faculty members and many other professionals, in contrast, expect to plateau rather early in their career and do not automatically feel stuck. It is only when we apply a corporate model of upward mobility that the career plateau takes on a negative connotation—which does not mean that there are no major challenges inherent in remaining professionally vital when no career advancement incentives are available or that faculty do not often feel stuck and stagnant when they enter their senior years. These issues are critical in identifying strategies for enhancing faculty vitality, but it is not career plateauing itself that is the inherent source of these problems.

In short, without the support of senior faculty members, our collegiate institutions are unlikely to change significantly until the first part of the next century, after these faculty members have retired. This period of time is much too long to wait for change and revitalization. The stability of senior faculty members need not be considered an impediment to change; rather, stability serves as an essential anchor for any institution undergoing change. Senior faculty remind change agents in their institutions of underlying values and traditions that should not be sacrificed for the sake of expedience.

Senior faculty should never be considered impervious to change and innovation. Rather, they must be approached and brought into the process of change through a full understanding and appreciation of their distinctive needs, concerns, and perspectives. This monograph is intended to provide this understanding and to evoke a deeper appreciation of the rich resources that senior faculty can bring to their own revitalization and to the revitalization of their institutions.

Without the support of senior faculty, collegiate institutions are unlikely to change significantly until after these faculty have retired...too long to wait for change.

THE CASE OF STEPHEN ABBOT

To bring to life the issues of faculty vitality and ways in which institutions can fully engage their senior faculty, we invited Joseph Axelrod to reprise his case study of Stephen Abbot, a disguised university professor on a real college campus. Stephen Abbot has already been profiled twice in books about American higher education, first as a young faculty member during the turbulent and innovative 1960s and early 1970s in *The University Teacher as Artist* (Axelrod 1973) and later as a faculty member in midlife during the late 1970s in *Improving Teaching Styles* (Axelrod 1980). In this monograph, Stephen Abbot is in his senior years, facing the challenges of the 1990s. Much as John Updike has captured the essence of three different eras in recent American history and three different stages of life in his three books on Rabbit Angstrom (1960, 1971, 1990), Joseph Axelrod provides American higher education with three insightful portraits of one faculty member at three different points in the history of American higher education and at three different points in his own life.

Abbot is not presented here as a typical faculty member, for there is no such thing. Nor is he meant to represent the ideal or the troubled faculty member. Rather, it is hoped this one story will help readers imagine the many ways faculty life can unfold, and the multiple individual, institutional, and broader external features that affect the productivity of that life. These features that affect faculty productivity are the focus of the rest of this monograph.

The Student Years at Chicago (1947–1959)

Whenever Stephen Abbot thinks about his student years, he sees how his own college experiences influenced his career as a college teacher. He was an undergraduate at Chicago from 1947 to 1950—the golden years of what later came to be known at "the Hutchins College." Those three years of his life, from ages 16 to 19, were also golden years for Abbot. No one who took part in the life of the Hutchins College, it seems, can forget it. George Steiner (1989), noted critic and a friend of Abbot's during their freshman year, describes vividly in a *New Yorker* sketch "the intellectual exhilaration, the passionate electricity of spirit, that . . . made the University of Chicago under Hutchins the best there was" (p. 142). Beyond the heady atmosphere in the college, the teenage Abbot felt a special excitement everywhere he moved on the Chicago campus during the late 1940s. The war was over, and a new bright world was coming into being. It was a wonderful time to be a college student, and Abbot loved it.

In spring 1950, a few months before he was to be awarded the B.A., a major event took place in the 19-year-old's life. He was seen sharing a marijuana cigarette with a classmate, and the event was promptly reported. The classmate, a repeat offender, was expelled, but for Abbot, an enlightened Dean Bergman designed a much different penalty: weekly sessions for the entire summer at the Counseling Center, the famous clinic that Carl Rogers had established and was directing on campus. "Those sessions," Abbot later said, "were fascinating, and—believe it or not—they later influenced my teaching in profound ways."

That influence was not to become evident to Abbot for about two decades, however. Another Chicago influence played a more immediate and visible role: the powerful relationship with John Bergman that began that summer—a friendship that deepened with each passing year. In the early 1950s, Bergman left Chicago to take a top deanship at San Francisco State College, and it was he who later persuaded Abbot to come to California.

Abbot made the move in 1959, his fresh Chicago Ph.D. in hand, ready to assume his new teaching post at San Francisco State. He arrived precisely on John Dewey's one hundredth birthday! Bergman had studied with Dewey at Columbia, and during Abbot's frequent visits to the Bergmans in the 1950s, he and his mentor held long conversations about Dewey, together studying his writings on aesthetics and education. Those talks had a significant influence on Abbot's teaching style in later years.

The year of Abbot's move to San Francisco is symbolic in another way: 1959 marks the end of a stabler epoch in American higher education. That year saw the American government's response to the incredible news of the Russian *Sputnik*. Unbelievable grants and contracts were channeled to colleges and universities across the country, and the Federal Grant University (to use Clark Kerr's phrase) came into being. At the same time, in the late 1950s, state master plans to guide the future growth of higher education were also just being developed. The first of them, California's, was put in place in 1960.

It was at the end of the 1950s, too, that the attitudes of college students toward their studies changed radically. The students of the early 1950s were everywhere described as "apathetic." They studied hard enough but managed never to become involved either in their studies or in the problems with which society was then confronted. By the end of the decade, however, apathy gave way to activism. On his arrival at San Francisco State, Abbot learned that a large group of students had demonstrated against the House Un-American Activities Committee. The notorious HUAC was then in session at the San Francisco City Hall. Hundreds of students were washed down the marble steps of City Hall by policemen wielding fire hoses. And it was at about this time, too, that a statement of "Student Concerns" was solemnly presented by Berkeley students to the university's administration.

It was not until the mid-1960s, however, that Steve Abbot grasped the deep significance of these events.

An Explosive Decade (1959–1969)

At San Francisco State, Abbot met a dozen or more faculty members who had been undergraduates in the Hutchins College. Like John Bergman, they had been attracted to San Francisco State because the new president there had, for about a decade, been introducing reforms that followed the Chicago college model. He abolished the 60 or more academic departments and, in their place, established six broad-area "divisions." He encouraged the faculty to redefine every aspect of general education and to build interdisciplinary courses that would fit the new definitions.

In these beginning years of his teaching career, Abbot modeled his teaching almost entirely on the behavior of his own professors of literature. His image of himself strongly resembled his memory of them. His job as a teacher of literature was to teach *literature*. He knew, of course, that he was teaching students, but during these early years—until about 1964—the focus of his attention was placed on the subject matter of his courses.

His goal was simple and direct. He tried to transmit to his students some insights into the meanings of the world's major literary works and to place those works and their authors in the world's major cultural traditions. Abbot's professors had not ventured outside the western canon, but his division chair at San Francisco State suggested that, because he was now located on the "Pacific Rim" (a new term to him), he should include one or two Asian works in his courses.

While his graduate professors had mainly delivered lectures, the Hutchins College faculty had encouraged lively class discussion. Now, too, although he lectured occasionally, Abbot thought that his students learned better if they were active in the class. As a discussion leader, Abbot saw his responsibilities clearly: Keep the discussion moving, select which topics would be covered, decide when to introduce each one, summarize the topics already discussed. Above all, avoid tangential issues, making certain that all the important questions were covered. During his first years of teaching, Abbot never for a moment considered that the class as a whole, or any student in it, might wish—or should be asked—to undertake any of the responsibilities he had assigned to himself. He was the teacher, and it was his duty to play the teacher role.

Although Abbot liked his students, the general atmosphere in his classroom was impersonal. He was not deeply interested in his students as individuals; in an important sense he did not "care" about them as people. In those years, many professors were beginning to use first names when addressing students, especially in small-group discussion classes, but Abbot used only last names. And of course no student could, at that time, have called him "Steve."

In this first stage of Abbot's teaching, the course—its shape and its contents—was primary. If someone wanted to have a statement of what your course was about, you would show them your list of required readings. Nothing more needed to be said.

But sometime around 1964, this view changed. The shift was brought sharply into focus by the Free Speech Movement at Berkeley. The proclamations and demonstrations by students brought Abbot new insights about his job as a college teacher. His task, he now felt, was to teach *students.* He went on teaching them literature, of course, but his emphasis was now the individual student rather than the subject matter. His students responded enthusiastically to this shift in emphasis, and the atmosphere in his classroom became more personal.

Still, the whole enterprise was primarily intellectual. As Abbot would see later, his attention was not yet focused on the *whole* student but rather emphasized the development of linguistic and linear modes of perception. Analysis was the dominant mode of communication. A student's "intuition" about the meaning of a literary text was not rejected out of hand, but Abbot insisted that it had to be tested. He taught students how to look for evidence, how to read data, how to set one's starting points, and how to become aware of the terms of one's own (or a critic's) dialectic. In his advanced classes, he taught students how to search the text for subtle clues to the author's *intention*. That intention remained at the center of what followed: an interpretation of the work and, then, a judgment of the work. The process was complex but also crisp and clear. It could not be mastered without a great deal of practice. Abbot insisted that his students were being taught a rigorous "discipline." Together, they mastered a set of tools, learned a private language, underwent a common ritual. As a consequence, there developed between them a strong bond. They loved it.

The tumultuous events of 1968—the student and faculty strikes at San Francisco State—drew students even closer together. Abbot joined those of his colleagues (a majority in the School of Humanities) who were polarized to the left. Refusing to cross the picket line, Abbot remained in close contact with all his students, and they with one another, through the telephone network that the strikers set up in the basement of Ecumenical House, and Abbot's classes met regularly off campus during those hectic months.

The Quest Continues (1969–1979)
Despite the terrible disruptions of 1968 at San Francisco State, Abbot was optimistic about the future of higher education in America. At the beginning of the 1970s, however, he became aware that he was once again altering his view of what a college teacher should be. By spring 1970, when the invasion of Cambodia and the tragic killing of students at Kent State and Jackson State took place, he realized that his philosophy of education had changed. He now believed that college and university teachers, if they hoped to be effective in any profound way, had to look upon a student as a whole person, not merely as a "mind" to be trained.

This realization influenced Abbot's professional life in fundamental ways. His teaching was now based on an entirely different notion of what students *are*. The atmosphere in his classroom became intensely personalized. He became a learner along with his students. He was a more experienced learner, to be sure, but the difference was one of degree and not of kind. He wanted students to see him as a pursuer of knowledge rather than as a master of it.

In moving to these new attitudes toward himself, his discipline, and his students, Abbot went through some complex philosophical changes. He now believed that his emphasis on intellectual development and rational activity had been based on a false principle, and he realized that intellectual development could not be split from other aspects of the human personality. This shift in principles, translated into classroom practice, led to a whole new ethos in Abbot's classes. "Caring" became a central responsibility for every member of the group. Steve, as his students came to call him, was not only their teacher and severest critic; he was also, and above all, their friend. And some of his students from those years are still personal friends.

In his courses in literature, Abbot wanted the subject matter to serve his students in their growth as *people* and to confirm them in their status as adults. He wanted literature to become a natural part of their lives. He did not want it to remain something that they did for school and would want to stop doing as soon as they earned a degree. And there was another purpose. When students took the initiative and started a discussion at home about a novel they were reading for Abbot's class, something subtle happened: They were making a public statement about their commitment to literature.

During the early 1970s, Abbot developed a whole series of techniques that helped him achieve success in his work with students as people. He designed new formats for examinations that removed the motivation (and the opportunity) for cheating. His guidelines for term projects introduced an emphasis on nontraditional topics to combat the irrelevance of traditional term papers. His writing assignments were daring and exciting. He adopted a "workshop" approach to class discussion. Above all, he conveyed trust and he built trust. It was clear to students from their first hour in his class that this was not the place for game playing or ego trips. Abbot was happy in his work. He felt close to his students and they to him.

As the decade moved into its second half, however, Abbot began to feel that things were not quite right. For one thing, the curricular reforms of the 1960s that he had so vigorously supported were beginning to crumble, not only on his own campus but all over the country. Moreover, a new kind of student was beginning to appear in the universities, and this new student, it was evident, felt no responsibility and no sense of commitment to academic pursuits or to society. The "Me Generation" had arrived. Abbot's teaching style began to shift. A new kind of relationship was required for dealing with this new kind of student.

The Middle Years (1979–1989)

The late 1970s were not happy years for Stephen Abbot. He felt he had lost touch with his students, and his campus life depressed him. Moreover, during those years, his personal life fell apart, and his marriage ended in an amicable divorce. He met the crisis admirably. During the early years of the new decade, his personal life came together again, but his depression about the state of higher education in America remained with him for a long time. This feeling lasted for almost a whole decade, running through most of the Reagan years.

Abbot was convinced that a counterrevolution in higher education had taken place. It was not simply that the reforms of the 1960s had not lasted. What astonished him was that they had disappeared so very quickly. Abbot came to feel that he had somehow been tricked into joining the counterrevolutionaries. Why and how he did not know. The counterrevolution had already succeeded before he knew what was happening.

As the months and years passed, he resigned himself to the knowledge that the reactionary forces had won. Their first step had been to *strengthen* higher education in America. Decision makers throughout the nation strongly supported the colleges and universities. Everywhere minority youth (and white underclass youth as well) were being encouraged to complete their secondary education and go to college. At the same time, the second stage in the strategy was being implemented. The major historic goal of undergraduate education was being subverted. That historic goal was to *educate* young people—to give them the tools to help enrich their lives, make sound decisions for the years to come, bring up their children wisely, work actively in the community, participate more intelligently in political affairs. But now the colleges were being turned into *training* centers whose sole purpose was to prepare young people to serve government, business, and industry.

Abbot saw all of the decision-making bodies working together to make certain their two-step strategy would succeed. He would count them off on his fingers: the state legislatures and other government bodies, the college and university governing boards and their appointees, the accrediting agencies (especially the specialized agencies representing the professions that served the corporate world), the Washington-based higher education societies, the foundations and think tanks, and, of course, the corporate world. The new goal for higher education was not even disguised. It went under the name of "career education," and its appeal to students from middle- and lower-class families was built on a single principle: The whole point of your going to college is to earn more money.

Abbot's friends argued that there simply had never really been a "revolution" at all. Some victories had been won, to be sure, in such domains as student rights and faculty rights, unionization, and affirmative action. But all the curricular reforms of the 1960s, they pointed out, were changes introduced to meet temporary conditions. As soon as the enthusiasm of the reformers waned, the whole *system* simply rejected the changes and the old and more comfortable structures reappeared.

Abbot did not know whether he was right or they were. But of one thing he was certain: Whatever the cause, he was deeply disturbed by a new brand of student now filling his classes. It appeared to him that they resisted being given any responsibility for undertaking their own education. He felt students did not want him to pose problems for them to work: They simply wanted him to give the answers they could memorize. Sometimes he wondered whether they were not really interested in learning anything at all. On Abbot's campus, the dormitories, which had remained partially empty during the first years of the 1970s, were now once again full to bursting, and their occupants were noisy, high-spirited, and fun-loving.

The old dilemma—how much of his virtually absolute power in the classroom did he want to delegate to students?—now demanded a new answer. The students appearing in his classes did not *want* any of that power. Most of them, it seemed to Abbot, were happy to remain totally passive and to do as they were told; they certainly made no effort to become involved in the materials presented to them. Abbot gradually found himself forced to adopt classroom behaviors that were far removed from his teaching style of the late 1960s and early 1970s. And as the nation moved into the Reagan years, he felt increasingly that his relationship with his students bore a marked resemblance to the relationship his own professors had had with him when, as a graduate student, he sat passively in their classes, listening to their long (and often dreary) lectures.

What saved him during this period were the few students in each class who were devoted to him. As for the others, most of them simply lost their individual identity. As he faced them from the podium, they were just a sea of faces. Often, when he lectured, he would make eye contact with first one, then another. But his interest was no longer centered on his students. His attention was centered now, as in the early days of teaching, on his subject matter, the literary works themselves. His rather formal lectures for the most part focused on himself; it was his own insights, his own modes of perception, his own ideas that he lectured about.

He no longer expected students in his classes to come to know one another, exchange telephone numbers, make contact outside of class, and phone one another when there were problems they ran into. That belonged to a bygone age. Now, things were different. Occasionally, students telephoned him to explain why they would have to miss class that day, and he was pleased about that. But he found intolerable the question that usually followed: "Will you be doing anything important in class today?" He tried to see such matters with good humor and to imagine himself a student at San Francisco State—perhaps going to school full time and also working full time. While he was aware that many of his students were meeting such demanding schedules, he actually knew very little about their lives. A decade earlier, he would have collected background data on all his students. But now, such personal contact was limited to the very small group of students who stayed after class to chat or came to his office.

Even when Abbot had good rapport with his brighter students, however, the truth was that their thoughts had little importance for him. When he used ideas expressed by his students, it was for the sake of highlighting his own ideas. All of his conversations with students—before, during, or after class, or during his office hours—began with *his* ideas and sooner or later returned to him and his ideas. He always remained at the center.

During these years, from the late 1970s to the late 1980s, he never actually sat down to ask himself whether he was happy in his teaching job. Of course he was happy, he would have said. But there was a current of dissatisfaction that he often felt and pushed away. Except for his handful of devotees, he knew that he was out of touch with his students. Was it, possibly, generational? He was now in his 50s and judged his students (aside from a handful of "reentry students") to range from 18 to 25. He found them intelligent. They usually laughed when he said something funny, and a good many of them seemed to understand a good deal of what he was saying. But it was obvious to him that they just did not find his world very real.

Abbot did not believe the difficulty lay in his teaching style. He could not, in any case, go back to a student-centered discussion format—whether the crisp, intellectual model he followed in the late 1960s or the laid-back, "whole-person" model he followed in the 1970s. Aside from his overlarge classes, which could not accommodate a true discussion format, the times were no longer right for those student-centered modes. The style he was now following—with the focus on the subject matter but centered on *his* ideas and *his* personality—seemed the right one for him. That was clear. But now he must find a way to reconnect with his students.

At this time, Abbot was also feeling another, rather different source of disturbance. Through the years of the Reagan presidency (1981 through 1989), San Francisco State seemed to Stephen Abbot to become increasingly fragmented. Some colleagues who felt likewise said the reason was obvious. San Francisco State, they said, wanted to become a research university and, increasingly, the new faculty members being recruited were well-known specialists in one narrow field. Most of these experts were not interested in talking to colleagues in other departments. But their appearances on the "McNeil-Lehrer News Hour" were discussed in detail at the University Club's cocktail hour. And everyone agreed they were good for the school's image, even if they did not do much to contribute to a sense of "campus community."

Abbot found that these observations, accurate though they might be, were themselves symptoms rather than causes of what disturbed him. And those colleagues who blamed it all on "reverse discrimination" Abbot found intolerable. One of them pointed out that his department chair was now a woman; so were his school dean and the assistant dean, and so was the academic vice president.

For Abbot, the explanation of his disturbance lay elsewhere; the phrase to focus on, he said, was the *not caring*. He felt strongly about that. At one time he had seen his campus as a community of scholars who loved learning, as a community of concerned individuals who cared about one another. He hoped that at some point the pendulum would swing back and that that image would become reality once again. But with each passing year, the image of the community of scholars faded farther and farther away. And during the late Reagan years, he began to feel that it would never return.

The Late Years (1989–1999)

One must never say "never." The precise point when his classroom style took another turn came early in summer 1990. One day he realized suddenly that he was about to take a new "beginning"—that some kind of "recursive" movement was happening. It started when, as he was reviewing and revising his lecture notes for the fall semester, he suddenly found himself caught in the swift currents of "postmodernism." He had been reading the work of Richard Rorty, whom he had known quite well when they were classmates at Chicago, and he struggled for some months with these powerful new ideas. Then, when the school year opened, he was not quite ready for it. He faced a dilemma. It was not possible for him to go back to the old lecture notes. His old answers no longer satisfied him, and he did not yet have new ones. So he made a daring decision. He would share his "in-process" explorations with his students.

In the first meeting of his senior seminar, he laid it all out. He told his students what his problem was and how it arose. He told them he was groping his way. He used the metaphor of a journey and asked them to join him. He suggested that those who wanted a more traditional course should drop the course that very day and sign up for another section of the seminar. It was a dramatic beginning.

He compared notes with colleagues who were undergoing similar explorations. Some were planning new courses whose titles would begin with "postmodernism and . . . " or end with " . . . and the postmodern world." After a few weeks, Abbot knew that something important was happening in his class. At first he was not sure what. But it soon became clear to him that many students were sending him a signal that carried a message: "We're excited. Something important is happening here."

Something else important was also happening all around him during this period in his life. Everybody was going on-line, surfing the Web, "talking" to strangers in Ankara or Kyoto via e-mail. Abbot became aware that many colleagues were deeply attracted to the new technology. Some met their classes in rooms with a computer at every "student station." While he is not ready for this much technology, he would have welcomed some device students could hold in their hands during his lectures that would let him know (by glancing at a control board) how many members of the class were confused or bored or wanted more detail about the topic under discussion.

As for his search for the "right" teaching style, it seems to have come to an end. He is now convinced that every style is "right" so long as instructors and their students are sincere learners and remain open with one another. Trust is the key. If *caring* is there, on both sides, then it does not make any difference which teaching model you follow.

In 1996, Abbot entered an early retirement program available to California university faculty members. Now, working half time, he feels fairly comfortable. He is involved in his research project on postmodernism, and he is looking forward to full retirement in 1999. By summer of that year, he will have served California higher education for four full decades. In that same year, San Francisco State will celebrate its 100th birthday. There will be celebrations to mark both events, and Abbot looks forward to participating in them. The year 1999 also marks the centenary of the birth of Robert M. Hutchins, and Abbot hopes to join many other members of the Chicago class of 1950 to celebrate that centennial.

Today Abbot is relatively happy. Of course, he is disturbed by world events, the increasing pressure to abandon affirmative action, and the growing gap between rich and poor. He is concerned about the future of the human race but readily admits he might be unduly pessimistic. One must never say "never."

THE PRODUCTIVITY OF SENIOR FACULTY

When the character Stephen Abbot was first presented in 1973, Abbot was a prototype for Axelrod's description and discovery of a new approach to teaching, one that would be responsive to the shifting needs and interests of the activist students of the late 1960s and early 1970s. Abbot was young, idealistic, and perfectly suited to his time. His "outmoded" notions about education and instruction were changing, just as were San Francisco State University and the students attending it. Personal change matched perfectly with institutional change.

We are offered a second view of Stephen Abbot in the early 1980s, and we see a quite different person. Abbot is now in his early 40s, and the institution where he works is no longer at the forefront of innovation. Words of a more managerial tone, such as "educational outcomes" and "accountability," replace the language of educational reform ("student-centered learning" and "experiential education") that saturated and animated Abbot's life and the life of his students and faculty colleagues during the late 1960s and early 1970s. Abbot has grown older and perhaps wiser. He certainly is more skeptical and less naive about the political realities of higher education in his state and nation.

In this monograph, we meet Stephen Abbot for a third time. He has passed through his 50s and lived through additional changes in his institution and American higher education in the 1980s and early 1990s. He is surrounded by even more stridently managerial and political language—"budget shortfalls" and "retrenchment." For a while, he lost touch with most of his students, but now, in his 60s, he is once again trying new teaching approaches and excited by and committed to his teaching. Through it all, Stephen Abbot somehow retained a spirit, a thoughtful perspective, and a sense of vitality, and they are what make Stephen Abbot, and other senior faculty like him who have remained vital, such valuable assets to their institutions as they prepare for the new century.

Though brief and certainly unique in many ways, the portrait of Stephen Abbot is exceptional. It is the only published longitudinal case study of a single faculty member over a 40-year period. There are many lessons to be learned from this case study, as we shall note throughout this monograph. Two of the most important lessons, however, are particularly timely. First, institutions can no longer afford to

Institutions can no longer afford to take a laissez-faire approach to faculty vitality.

take a laissez-faire approach to faculty vitality, as appeared
to be the case with Abbot. The institutional—and broader—
environment clearly affects productivity and, when possible,
should be managed to have a positive effect. The second
lesson concerns the deep wisdom that Abbot has acquired
over the past 40 years and the very real possibility that the
leaders of his institution will never take advantage of it.
Without the wisdom of Stephen Abbot—and the many other
senior faculty members in his university and other colleges
and universities in this country—we will be ill-prepared for
the challenges we now face.

The Challenge for Senior Faculty

As we try to make sense of Stephen Abbot's story and the
stories of other senior faculty who have lived through these
same major transitions in American higher education, we
face shifting notions about what it means to be successful as
a faculty member and what one must do to be successful. By
the time most faculty members of Abbot's era reached their
late 40s and early 50s, they envisioned themselves as having
"made it" through the traditional academic career paths, or
as having accumulated the resources and network to still
"make it"—sometimes through alternative pathways. Alternatively, they have plateaued and are no longer interested
in, or no longer hold much hope of, additional career advancement. In either case, senior faculty are freed to make
choices regarding the direction of their research, scholarship,
teaching, organizational role, and, more generally, career.

To be free from constraints, however, does not necessarily mean that one knows what to do with this freedom
(Bergquist and Weiss 1994). Freedom is often quite frightening, especially for someone who has lived for many years
with real (or imagined) career constraints. As long as one
has to publish to survive, or teach in a certain manner to
gain senior colleagues' acceptance, or perform certain roles
and provide certain services in the institution to gain tenure,
then one need not question the wisdom of the choices made
about research, teaching, or institutional role. Now, however, senior faculty like Stephen Abbot have choices to
make—at a time in life when there are often reasons for
both hope and despair. So much depends on how senior
faculty choose to frame their experiences and the new (or
old) ways in which they choose to lead their lives.

This is a time of life and a point in one's career when one asks questions about relevance (Braskamp et al. 1982). The answers will vary widely among senior faculty, for they are no longer constrained by a single set of confining standards that confronted them at an earlier age when they sought promotion and tenure. "Professors vary considerably in how they live their professional [lives]" (p. 22). Some of the senior faculty that Braskamp and his colleagues studied tend to focus inward—toward integration: "As they are getting settled as full professors, they write the integrative piece in their field or apply their knowledge in new settings. As they near the end of the professional career, they strive to write the masterpiece to encompass their life's work, to assist others in furthering work begun by them, and to play the role of the elder statesperson" (p. 22). Others, however, use this time in life to branch out—to move away from their former activities, "to pursue new interests[, such as] consulting [and] public speaking, [to] rekindle old interests . . . , and to spend more time with their family. They were satisfied with the level of performance when promoted and were willing to maintain it rather than enhance it" (p. 22).

Obviously, senior faculty members' activities vary widely, making it is very difficult to portray the productivity of senior faculty. Further, what is considered productive at one institution is not at another. Stephen Abbot comes from an institution that has always encouraged excellence in teaching as well as scholarly productivity or research. Some institutions would not require the scholarship or research; others would not be as concerned about instruction. Thus, the faculty member who excels at a balanced approach (one article a year, new innovations in his or her courses each year, consistent outreach activities, and participation on one university committee) might be considered highly productive at a comprehensive institution but a low producer at a research university. And "breaking down academic work into separate roles and finer and finer phases may miss the essence of work in academia. Analyzing the parts may not produce an understanding of the whole" (Blackburn 1974, p. 76).

Nevertheless, some are concerned that senior faculty may not be as productive. Some of this concern has been based on a belief that senior faculty are not mentally able to maintain the necessary level of content knowledge and skills. But most longitudinal studies find no consistent decline in cognitive functions until the 60s, and many adults retain high abilities until much older. Even in the 50s, the "average" decline observed is not caused by aging, but by diseases that affect only a small minority of people (Bray and Howard 1983; Schaie 1983; Siegler 1983; Willis and Tosti-Vasey 1990). For most people in the studies, mental abilities were constant over time.

In fact, abilities that are used often do not peak until mid-life. A review of the biological literature on the impact of age on intelligence notes that the decline resulting from age is quite modest well into the 70s for people with no major diseases (Kallio and Ging 1985). The decline is least for "those with a positive socioeconomic status (or stimulating environment), those who manifested a flexible personality style in middle years, and those who manifest greater initial intelligence. [And because] faculty generally possess all three of [these] characteristics, they may be expected to experience even less decline in intelligence than the general population" (p. 11). Another review of research on age and expertise reveals that new professionals have a rather fractured and not well organized cognitive structure, while experienced professionals typically have well integrated and highly organized knowledge bases that allow them to quickly fold in new knowledge and solve problems (Willis and Tosti-Vasey 1990).

The concern about senior faculty members' productivity became apparent with the uncapping of the mandatory retirement age, and a flurry of articles appeared on "what to do" about the aging professoriat and the productivity of older faculty members. Again, it was frequently assumed that older faculty would be, because of age, less productive (Baldwin and Blackburn 1981; Hodgkinson 1974). Is this assessment accurate for most senior faculty? Was it true of Stephen Abbot? To address these complex concerns, this section summarizes the literature on senior faculty and their productivity in the areas of teaching, research, and service. As the reader will soon learn, some decline in productivity might occur as faculty age, but age itself is not a major predictor of productivity and other factors have a much greater impact. The factors that affect the vitality of all faculty also affect senior faculty: for example, motivation, competence, appreciation, rewards, and climate. As the next section, "Looking Inside for Vitality," notes, some of these factors are of particular importance to senior faculty (e.g., appreciation), while others (e.g., rewards) are of relatively less importance.

Several researchers on age versus productivity suggest their findings "clearly point to the need for more sophisticated analyses of cause-effect relationships between individual and institutional variables and career patterns" (Lawrence and Blackburn 1985, pp. 151–52). This theme of the intimate interplay of individual variables and institutional variables on faculty members' vitality is persistent across all the literature, and the concluding sections of this monograph on fostering faculty vitality return to it. But first, what do we know from the literature about the productivity of senior faculty members, and how do these findings relate to what we know about the vitality of Stephen Abbot and other senior faculty?

Teaching

Studies find that senior faculty commit about the same amount of time to teaching as younger faculty and that almost all have some student advisees; moreover, senior faculty list teaching as a priority (El-Khawas 1991). Several studies find that interest in teaching increases with age (Baldwin and Blackburn 1981; El-Khawas 1991). Thus, concerns about senior faculty's no longer being interested in or committed to students or to teaching are unfounded.

The findings are mixed with regard to the competencies of senior faculty members as teachers when compared to younger faculty. Small positive correlations were found between academic rank and teaching effectiveness in a group of studies conducted over a 30-year period, but the rank of full professor encompasses 30 to 40 years, making it difficult to generalize (Blackburn and Lawrence 1986). Other studies have found that a low-order negative correlation exists between age and the effectiveness of teaching in the college classroom. Younger teachers typically are rated higher than older teachers. A study of student ratings among 70 college faculty found that age was negatively related to teaching effectiveness (Cornwell 1974), while another found a negative relationship between student ratings and number of years since receiving a doctorate (Linsky and Straus 1975). The relationship between age and teaching performance, however, is not great. One study, for instance, found that age accounted for only 6 percent of the variance in students' ratings (Cornwell 1974).

One of the few longitudinal studies that has been performed (Heilman and Armentrout 1936) yielded results suggesting stable ratings of instruction over a seven-year period. This very dated study has been replicated in our own time (Horner, Murray, and Rushton 1989), examining students' ratings for 106 full-time faculty members in psychology over a two- to 15-year period. It found an overall negative correlation of .33 between age and general teaching effectiveness and similar correlations between age and specific measures of teaching effectiveness. The authors offer several ideas regarding the reasons for this decline.

First, they suggest that biological processes slow down as one ages, accompanied by a personality change that is detrimental to teaching (Horner, Murray, and Rushton 1989, p. 228). Citing the argument that senior faculty find few rewards for effective teaching, especially because in most instances they are tenured and at the highest position in the institution (full professor) (Blackburn and Lawrence 1986), they suggest that the decline in teaching performance may relate to generational differences rather than age. Older faculty are more likely to experience a gap between their own life experiences and those of their students. While this "generation gap" may narrow and even reverse when a faculty member is teaching an older group of students, the gap is likely to remain a detriment for most faculty until such time as a majority of students in collegiate institutions are over 45 years of age.

The self-fulfilling prophecies associated with stereotyping people by race, gender, ethnicity, physical abilities—and age—are another factor (Horner, Murray, and Rushton 1989). If members of a collegiate institution—in particular, students —assume that senior faculty are "burned out," dated, and far removed from contemporary problems, then the faculty will not be of much interest or use as teachers. Senior faculty will in turn feel unappreciated, they will find it hard to motivate students, and they will usually be assigned to teach the traditional courses (because they are supposedly "out-of-date"). Under such conditions, senior faculty are likely to become discouraged, unmotivated, and distant from students, thereby verifying the initially faulty assumptions that have been made. The strong disengagement that Stephen Abbot's students report in his senior years suggests that just such a self-fulfilling prophecy has occurred, at least temporarily, for him.

These mixed results and the variables involved make it difficult to arrive at firm conclusions about the relationship between age and teaching. Some studies have found that age discrimination does seem to negatively affect performance ratings (Clark 1992; Finkelstein 1982)—particularly when the people doing the rating are young and the person being rater is older, as would be the case for students rating senior faculty. Second, the studies that have been conducted are rarely longitudinal; as a result, we have no way of knowing whether the teaching performance is declining or this particular cohort of faculty members were always slightly less effective in the classroom. Perhaps new faculty members enter their jobs with greater commitment to teaching or with more training as teachers. With the decline in public support for higher education, many of our younger faculty members come with an expectation that higher education will probably never pay very well or even offer them much employment security. They are more likely to be motivated by a desire to teach rather than a search for job security (tenure) or high pay. Further, many universities today require training in teaching for their graduate students who are teaching assistants. Thus, new faculty are more likely to have formal training in teaching than senior faculty. Whether these changes in the attitudes, expectations, and training of young faculty translate into better teaching is another matter. Only further longitudinal studies will enable us to differentiate the issue of age from the issue of age cohort.

In summary, no studies found a large negative association between a faculty member's age and effective teaching. If a negative effect exists, it is small. It is clear, however, that senior faculty are interested in, committed to, and devote significant time to teaching.

Research
The first major study on faculty productivity as a function of age used entries in several histories of science as a criterion of successful contribution to the body of knowledge in a specific field (Lehman 1953). The study found that scientists completed the work being cited more often before they were 40 than after they were 40. Most subsequent studies concerned with the research productivity of faculty as a

function of age have reported this same difference—though with an initial low level of productivity when a faculty member is young.

This curvilinear relationship is commonly found, regardless of the criterion being used to define productivity or the discipline studied, although it should be noted that nearly all these studies were done on faculty in the sciences or social sciences (Cole 1979; Dennis 1956; Horner, Rushton, and Vernon 1986; Lehman 1966). Productivity tends to be fairly low when faculty are in their 20s, largely because they are still completing their requirements for advanced degrees, settling in as newly appointed faculty members, establishing their research setting (laboratory, library, subject pool, and so forth), and beginning to learn the subtle and often elusive arts of teaching and campus politics. Productivity tends to increase during the 30s, peak around age 40, and decline thereafter.

It was previously thought that the decrease in productivity was a result of a decline in energy, ideas, or cognitive abilities, or a result of the loss of external motivation (promotion and tenure). This general conclusion held sway in higher education for many years, but it has been challenged in recent years by several researchers. Some have noted that there were many more young faculty than older faculty during the time when many of the studies were done and that there is a greater tendency on the part of historians of science to focus on the early, breakthrough discoveries in faculty members' careers than on their later, substantiating work (Cole 1979; Dennis 1956).

Yet even when the size of the age cohort is taken into account and the criterion of productivity concerns number of publications rather than impact on one's discipline, a decline still occurs in the rate of productivity as a function of age (Cole 1979; Horner, Rushton, and Vernon 1986; Over 1982, 1988). "If fewer outstanding contributions come from older scientists, it may not be just because older scientists are fewer in number but because they have reduced research output" (Over 1989, p. 222; see also Over 1988).

It should be noted, however, that while these overall declines are true, age still accounts for only around 6 percent of the variance in research productivity (Horner, Rushton, and Vernon 1986; Over 1982). Great individual differences exist. For example, "high-level producers (those publishing more than one article per year and [accounting for] one-third of the sample), . . . even after decline . . . at 55 to 64 [were] . . . more productive than the remaining two-thirds of the sample had been at their peak" (Horner, Rushton, and Vernon 1986, p. 322).

The results, however, are still not definitive, for several other complex and confounding factors are involved. First, it is unclear exactly how the number of citations should be measured. Is high quality defined by the overall number of times the work of a faculty member is cited, or by the number of articles or books a faculty member has authored that are cited a certain number of times? While some evidence suggests that older faculty attract fewer citations than younger faculty (Cole 1979; Over 1982, 1989, pp. 222–23), other results suggest there is basically no difference between younger and older faculty with regard to citations per article (Oromaner 1977; Over 1988). Thus, younger faculty may have more citations than older faculty, but it may be the result of their higher production of articles and books overall than of their production of high-quality (frequently cited) work.

A key factor that leads to the confusion appears to be the intermingling of quality and quantity in the measurement of productivity. "Despite the general drop in research output with age [a quantitative criterion], the ratio of high-quality to low-quality publication [a qualitative criterion] remains relatively constant over the professional life span" (Simonton 1984, 1985, cited in Over 1989, p. 223). A study of the ratio of high- to low-quality articles finds that young faculty produce more high-quality articles (as defined by number of citations) than older faculty; however, they also produce more low-quality articles (Over 1988, 1989). The results are further confounded by the placement of articles in specific, highly visible journals (Oromaner 1977). Younger and older faculty attract similar rates of citation when articles published in the same journal are compared (Over 1982, 1989). Moreover, the variance in publication rate among faculty increases with age. It is not a consistent decline; rather, it appears many faculty remain highly productive, while others significantly reduce their publishing activity.

Finally, when productivity is measured by something other than number of citations, the outcome tends to change. Results from two national surveys of faculty in the late 1980s and one from the early 1970s suggest that "publication activity is reported by almost all senior faculty at four-year institutions, but by four in 10 senior faculty at two-year institutions" (El-Khawas 1991, p. 4). Specifically, the self-reports of faculty at four-year institutions in the two 1980s surveys indicate that 84 percent of senior faculty at four-year institutions had published articles in professional journals, 60 percent had published books, monographs, or manuals, and 45 percent had published chapters in edited books—much higher percentages than in the 1972–73 survey. The percentages for faculty at two-year institutions were lower—42 percent had published articles, 39 percent had published books, monographs, or manuals, and 10 percent had published chapters in edited books—but again, the percentages were higher than in 1972–73.

Unfortunately, these data tell us nothing about shifts in rates of productivity over the years, because they refer to total levels of productivity. While "the idea that senior faculty never publish is . . . contradicted" by this information (El-Khawas 1991, p. 10), the evidence points only to the fact that contemporary senior faculty have been more productive over their total careers than were their counterparts during the early 1970s. Nevertheless, these data suggest that other measures of productivity might be used rather than just citations and that such data probably already exist in the type of national surveys El-Khawas cites.

Four other flaws overarch and perhaps override many of the studies that have been conducted. First, most of the studies focus exclusively on faculty in the sciences and social sciences, specifically psychology. We know very little about changes in the rate of productivity among faculty in the humanities or arts. While some of the studies concern "scholarship" (e.g., Over 1982, 1989) rather than "research," virtually all of them focus on publication in refereed, disciplinary journals rather than on any other mode of dissemination (conferences, consultations, public reports, magazine articles, and so forth). In many disciplines, products are displayed primarily through exhibits at museums, showings at galleries, live performances, theatrical productions, and works of fiction. And what about instructional products (including textbooks and published case studies) and productions on the Internet? These other modes of productivity may be particularly important for senior faculty, who are often more inclined (and better positioned in their institutions) than their younger colleagues to communicate their ideas and insights through modes other than traditional, disciplinary journals.

Second, the studies primarily focus on four-year research universities, usually ignoring the work of senior faculty at liberal arts colleges and two-year community colleges, or using criteria of productivity (publication in major refereed journals or number of citations) that are strongly biased toward faculty with disciplinary connections and institutionally based access and reputation.

Third, the primary focus on number of citations does not satisfactorily address qualitative criteria, thus yielding not only a limited sample of research production, but also a dichotomous measure—either an article or book is cited or is not cited. Moreover, the citation does not take into account how often faculty members cite their own previous work or the function of delay; that is, some articles and books are seminal in their field yet are "discovered" much later than other seminal works.

Fourth, criteria regarding citation are confounded by changes in data-retrieval systems. The frequency with which works in some fields are cited may depend more on the extent and sophistication of bibliographic databases in their field than the importance of these works.

Finally, the conclusions from an extensive review of faculty productivity and age are worth noting:

> *When one takes into consideration the percentage of the productivity variance being accounted for by the age variable, good sense would say to some, set it aside. The relationships are so weak that if it were not for a strong, yet apparently ill-founded, faith that an age/ productivity relationship does exist and would be found if only one were smart enough to document it, one would table this line of inquiry and move on to a more profitable vein in order to mine for other factors affecting faculty productivity* (Blackburn and Lawrence 1986, p. 280).

Keeping in mind the problems with the previously noted studies as well as Blackburn and Lawrence's advice, we can say that quality in research seems to be more important than quantity for mature faculty members. Senior faculty may produce less, but what they do produce is at least comparable to that produced by younger faculty.

As with less effective teaching for senior faculty, several reasons may be offered for this apparent shift in priority from quantity to quality and the possible overall decline in quantity. First, as has been suggested by many who have studied the productivity of faculty, the concern for quality may result from the reduction in pressure for publication that comes with the tenure and promotional review of many collegiate institutions—especially four-year colleges and universities with at least a secondary emphasis on research. Senior faculty may have the experience and capacity to write integrative, synthetic works that they did not have as young academics. Years in a field, hearing many colleagues wrestle over time with enduring concepts, can greatly enhance the interpretation of fragmented individual studies through a meta-analysis.

In his exploration of new concepts in postmodernism, Stephen Abbot, like other senior faculty members, may make important contributions to his field. Abbot seems to be patient about coming to new insights and hence may allow these insights to fully mature before presenting them. Unlike his younger colleagues, Abbot can afford this luxury because he is not under the same pressure to publish.

The shifting priorities could also be a manifestation, quite simply, of the broader role that senior faculty play in the organization. We know that senior faculty have a larger time commitment to committees and are more likely to take on administrative roles. Thus, one picks the research one can focus on most profitably with less time, given the increased time devoted to other activities. Or it may be a result of the more general shift among mature men and women toward focusing more on those things about which they care deeply (Bergquist, Greenburg, and Klaum 1993). Senior faculty are inclined to discard all but the most important projects (research, scholarly reading and review, committee assignments, and so forth) so that they can truly care for those few projects that are most important and will yield the highest-quality products.

Given these several possible reasons for the shift in research priorities and the lower quantity of articles produced, the leaders of collegiate institutions might want to follow the suggestion that they intervene through mechanisms such as professional development and resource allocation to "increase the research output of older scientists without adversely affecting the quality of what they produce" (Over 1989, p. 225; see also Over 1982).

It appears that research funds often are not evenly shared among junior and senior faculty. A review of several national faculty surveys found that "senior faculty are somewhat less likely than other faculty to have research funds. Forty-four percent of senior faculty at four-year institutions reported having research funds, compared to 51 percent of all faculty at these institutions" (El-Khawas 1991, p. 6). It is quite understandable that junior faculty are given substantial support, for they are just starting out and are expected to be productive if they are to gain tenure and promotion. It is equally understandable that support for senior faculty is not forthcoming and that their own research initiatives are often ignored or taken for granted, given that they no longer need to publish so as not to "perish," their research initiatives are already well established, and their rate and style of productivity are already seemingly "entrenched." Nevertheless, "closer examination of the sources of this difference [in access to research funds] is warranted. Are institutional expectations and incentives skewed toward younger faculty?" (p. 10).

Collegiate leaders might wish to acknowledge the shifting priorities of senior faculty, paralleling the more general shift of mature adults away from quantity to selective quality and generative caring. Under these conditions, administrators might emphasize senior faculty members' efforts to produce high-quality work and to break down old habits (perhaps acquired during their years of publish or perish) of publishing large volumes of lower-quality work.

Service

No hard data have been found regarding the effectiveness of senior faculty in their roles as committee members, organizational problem solvers or conflict managers, contributors to their professional disciplines, or providers of outreach—a most unfortunate situation because these areas are where senior faculty play major roles and are much more likely than younger faculty to do so. Further, some research regarding aging faculty reveals that senior faculty members often can serve as valuable resources to the institution because they know the history of their discipline and institution and are able to appreciate more fully the context within which a problem resides than do their younger colleagues (Wheeler 1990). They tend to be respected by their colleagues, particularly if they have been successful in their field or in running some specific program at their college or university. In some instances, they also are judged by their colleagues to be more "objective" or at least in some sense detached from the daily politics of the institution. They tend to take a long-term, historical perspective and are concerned with the overall welfare of the institution—though under conditions of stagnation rather than generativity, they can be among the most vindictive and short-sighted of all faculty members (Wheeler 1990).

No evidence exists of a large decline in [faculty members'] effectiveness or productivity because of age.

Conclusions

Despite the fact that 50 percent of our full-time faculty will soon be over the age of 50, no evidence exists of a large decline in the effectiveness of their teaching or productivity in research because of age. Senior faculty continue to demonstrate interest in and commitment to teaching, commitment to quality in research, and commitment of time to organizational roles. One major theme in the writings that influences whether a faculty member will or will not be productive in the senior years, however, is the interplay between individual and institutional factors. Stephen Abbot continues to be productive in part because he has personally shifted his own activities in response to changing interests and values in his own life. His productivity has also been affected, both positively and negatively, by how he responded to the shifting environment of the institution where he works. Ultimately, faculty vitality is determined by how one responds to both personal and institutional changes.

LOOKING INSIDE FOR VITALITY:
Internal Factors Affecting the Productivity of Senior Faculty

It seems that faculty members' competence and productivity do not significantly decline as a function of age. The priorities of senior faculty do appear to change, however, as evidenced by such things as their focusing on quality rather than quantity in research, and their role as institutional leaders. While the particular stage of adult and career development for senior faculty like Stephen Abbot influences their vitality, they also continue to be influenced by factors associated with the vitality of all faculty members. Understanding the characteristics of productive faculty members, whatever their age, as well as those endemic to senior faculty can help one select new directions or changes in the institution that facilitate vitality.

This section summarizes the literature on internal factors associated with faculty vitality across all age groups. As an aid in understanding the possible shifts in priorities as we age, it focuses, in particular, on the literature about adult development as it specifically applies to faculty. The next section summarizes the literature on *external* factors associated with faculty vitality, across ages, and focuses on the literature about career development among faculty to further our understanding of external factors that influence the priorities of senior faculty. Each aspect of internal and external vitality is important, and addressing one alone is insufficient. All of the factors work together to provide the conditions necessary for faculty vitality (see figure 1).

Adult Development and the Shifting Priorities of Senior Faculty

As we grow older, our interest in, and perspectives on, various modes of productivity change. We like to do different things in our 50s and 60s from what we did in our 20s, and we aspire to different goals from those of our youth (Bergquist, Greenburg, and Klaum 1993). This is the central message to be conveyed by the research on adult development as we consider the factors inside senior faculty members that influence their productivity and vitality.

The discovery—or invention—of adulthood and adult stages of development in the behavioral sciences is significant, for it has shifted our notions about how to motivate and revitalize men and women between 21 and 65 years of age. We now know that people differ significantly with regard to needs and interests not only as a function of gender,

FIGURE 1

Components of a Productive Academic Organization

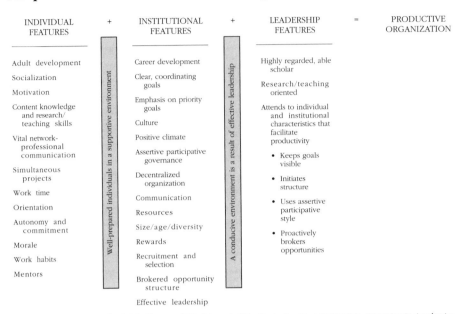

Source: Adapted from C.J. Bland, S.N. Chou, and T.L. Schwenk, "The Productive Organization," in *Managing in Academics: A Health Center Model*, edited by J. Ridky and G.F. Sheldon (St. Louis: Quality Medical Publishing, 1993), p. 28.

race, socioeconomic level, and abilities, but also as a function of age. As we look to ways for maintaining the vitality of senior faculty members in our colleges and universities, it is not surprising that we have recently looked to research and models of adult development for guidance.

While the notion of human development can be traced back almost a century to the work of Arnold van Gennep, Jose Ortega y Gasset, and Carl Jung, it has gained prominence and a stable theoretical base with the work of Swiss psychologist Jean Piaget (1896–1980) and German-born psychoanalyst Erik Erikson (1902–1994). Piaget (Inhelder and Piaget 1958) identified four specific sets of cognitive competencies that must be acquired in a sequential manner as children mature and become thoughtful and successful adults, and one must successfully achieve the cognitive competencies associated with one stage of the Piagetian model before proceeding to the next stage. At about the same time, Erikson (1985) described eight stages of life, from infancy through old age. Unlike Piaget, Erikson assumed that one

moves on to the next stage of development in life, regardless of one's level of success in the previous stage or stages.
In the Piagetian model, unsuccessful development results in
a person's being stuck at a specific stage of life. Conversely,
in the Eriksonian model, one carries developmental failures
forward in life, making success in each of the subsequent
stages more difficult as the continuous accumulation of failures becomes more damaging and difficult to overcome.

Eriksonian models of adult development

The first four of Erikson's developmental stages address the
issues of infancy and childhood, the last four adulthood. The
fifth stage concerns primarily the formation of identity as an
adult, and the building of a sense of continuity in life roles
and goals, while the sixth stage focuses on the capacity to
establish an intimate relationship and the formation of a lov-
ing relationship with another person. Generativity is central
to the seventh stage, with midlife adults concerned with
guidance of the next generation. The eighth and final stage
concerns primarily the integrity of one's life experiences and
the acceptance of one's own distinctive life cycle (see figure
2) (Erikson 1982).

The basic Eriksonian model has undergone two major extensions and modifications over the past two decades (Gilligan 1982; Levinson 1996; Levinson et al. 1978). Like Erikson,
Levinson addresses the life cycle, but his studies of the life
cycle in men (Levinson et al. 1978) and women (1996) focus
on the last three Eriksonian stages, specifically on the seventh stage (see figure 2). Within the seventh stage, Levinson
concentrates on the transitions associated with the early 40s,
expanding on Erikson's model by identifying both structure-
building periods and structure-changing or transitional periods within specific life-cycle eras. The crises and stress associated with transitional periods are normal aspects of the
developmental process and are to be differentiated from
"adaptive crises," which occur when a major traumatic event
occurs in one's life (such as combat, illness, or abuse).

Developmental crises may be very traumatic and demand
a reevaluation of one's priorities and needs, yet without
these crises and the structural changes they bring about,
men and women are likely to remain caught in their current
developmental stage and will be ill prepared for addressing
the age-related challenges of their next era in the life cycle.

FIGURE 2

Stages of Adult Development

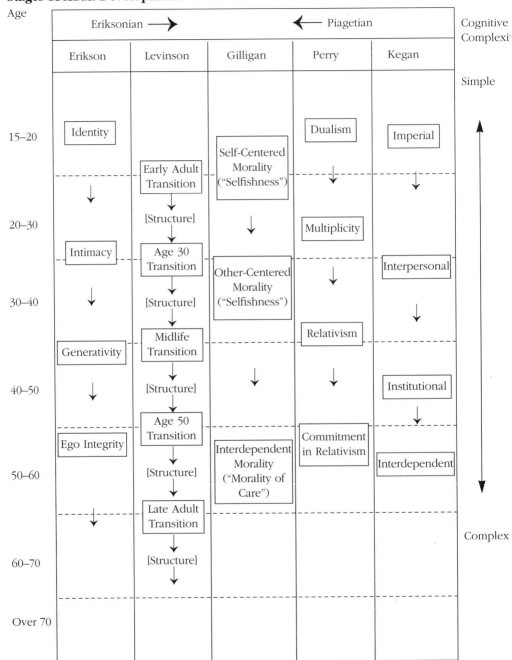

Originally, the midlife crisis was identified as the struggles of men and women in their late 40s who have never addressed the life changes inherent in their early 40s, not the normal and necessary transitions of the early 40s, that are the points of "crisis." It is the failure to address "midlife" issues that produces the "midlife" crisis, not the transitional period itself. This area is often misunderstood in the popular literature on adult development.

While Levinson built on the Eriksonian model by focusing on points of transition and, in particular, on midlife, Gilligan (1982) focuses primarily on differences between men and women in their movement through the life cycle. She suggests that the assumption in Erikson's model that one forms an identity in early adulthood preceding the formation of intimate relationships in middle adulthood may be distinctively male, noting that many women (and some men) forge their identities in conjunction with their experience of becoming intimate with another person. Moreover, she argues, Erikson overemphasizes a movement toward greater individuation and the clarification and reformulation of one's own personal identity independent of the specific context within which one lives. One's identity, after all, exists within a specific context, and maturation could be considered a movement toward mutuality of care rather than greater individuation (see figure 2).

Piagetian models of adult development

In keeping with the epistemological orientation of Piaget, most Piagetian models of adult development begin with a concept of unfolding or maturing cognitive structures and their impact on personal and interpersonal aspects of self (see figure 2). Kegan (1982), for instance, offers a six-stage theory of development that traces the maturation of the construction of meaning processes in one's life, believing that human development consists of a series of stages in which one's sense of self becomes increasingly differentiated from his or her sense of the external world.

A comparable model of adult development that relies on cognitive maturation (Loevinger, Wessler, and Redmore 1970), while clearly in the Piagetian camp, questions the Piagetian assumption that each stage builds on the previous stages and is somehow superior to them. Each stage "has its weaknesses, its problems, and its paradoxes, which provide both a potential for maladjustments and a potential for growth" (Loevinger 1966, p. 200).

Loevinger also focuses on the extent to which one is able to reason and make decisions independent of other people and, in particular, the dominant frames of reference offered by the society in which a person lives. In many ways, the research and theorizing of Gilligan and her colleagues take the concerns of Loevinger one step further. Not only are "higher" stages of cognitive development not necessarily better than lower stages, they also may represent a model of development that is neither descriptive of development in all people nor necessarily an appropriate source of normative guidelines.

Applying adult development theory to faculty

Hodgkinson (1974) was the first to apply adult development theory to understanding the stages of development among faculty (see figure 3). Although he used age as the source of differentiation between stages, Hodgkinson cautioned against the strict use of age as the basis for the stage of one's life. Particularly when it comes to the description of faculty, it is imperative that a theory of stages be flexible and that faculty and administrators who apply the theory to institutional policy and procedures not engage in self-fulfilling prophecies that impose inappropriate solutions on the distinctive problems confronted by individual faculty members.

Building on Levinson's model, Hodgkinson identifies seven stages of a faculty member's career (see figure 3), the first six stages encompassing the years before seniority: (1) getting into the adult world (ages 22–29), (2) age 30 transition (approximately 28–32), (3) settling down or moving up (30–55), (4) becoming one's own person (35–39), (5) middlescence (39–43) and (6) restabilization (43–50). He devotes little time to senior faculty—the seventh stage or later years—who, according to Hodgkinson, are becoming aware of their physical decline, beginning to prepare for retirement, and often experiencing great satisfaction in their career accomplishments.

Focusing on the transitions from assistant to associate and from associate to full professor, Braskamp and his colleagues applied Levinson's model in their analysis of interviews with 48 faculty at a major research university (Braskamp et al. 1982). They identified an initial career transition

FIGURE 3
Stages of Faculty and Career Development

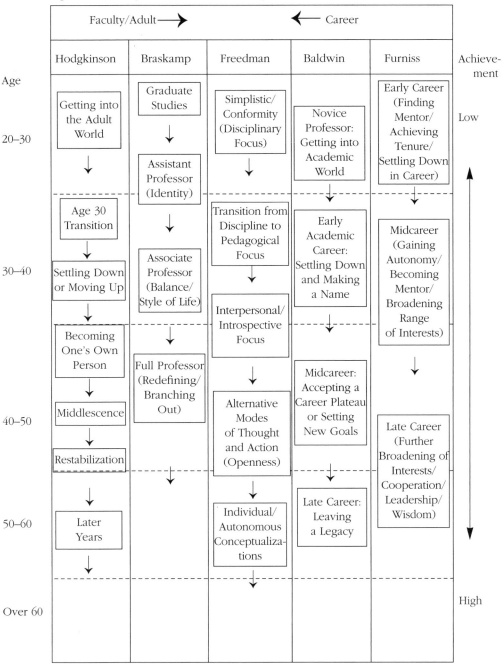

from graduate studies to assistant professorship and a period of relative stability and consolidation in which a faculty member enters his or her profession, establishes an identity as a professional, and attends to advancement in the profession, paralleling Levinson's pattern of major change followed by a period of relative stability.

A second transition occurs with the transition from assistant to associate professor, followed by establishing or reestablishing a balance in life, selecting a professional lifestyle, and seeking advancement to a higher position in the institution. The final stage is the transition from associate to full professor and the subsequent redefining of one's professional lifestyle, branching out into other areas of life and work, and fulfilling lifetime goals.

A summary of the research to the early 1980s on the interplay between faculty and adult development also extensively used Levinson's analysis in describing an age 30 transition, a midlife transition, and a senior career transition but also incorporated research on women's development, noting in particular that women often forge dual identities, one centered on career and the other on family (Cytrynbaum, Lee, and Wadner 1982). Moreover, the pulls between these two identities may be particularly salient for a female faculty member in a dual-career relationship.

A more recent survey of faculty and adult development models also borrows heavily from Levinson (D. Kelly 1991), noting that faculty during their senior years "may desire the opportunity to provide nurturing to other younger faculty. In addition, adults at this stage are likely to be interested in issues of health and retirement" (p. 6).

Although these four researchers (Hodgkinson, Braskamp, Cytrynbaum, and Kelly) offer excellent illustrations of the use of adult development theory to aid the planning of strategies for motivating and developing faculty, they all are to be faulted—like Levinson—for the lack of clarity regarding differences between the various stages of development after age 50. The senior years for faculty are a time for developing new dreams, building a legacy, and nurturing the next generation. The senior years are not just a time in which faculty prepare for retirement (as Hodgkinson, Cytrynbaum, and Kelly suggest). Preparation for retirement usually does not begin with the very late 50s or early 60s unless a faculty member is considering early retirement. Just as Hodgkinson

The senior years for faculty are a time for developing new dreams, building a legacy, and nurturing the next generation.

lumps together all the development issues after age 50 into a single stage, most Americans, whether studying adult development among older faculty members or preparing for their own 50s, 60s, and later, generally neglect or never discover the distinctive features of the senior years.

Most applications of adult development theory to faculty have borrowed primarily from the Eriksonian model of development and, more specifically, from Levinson's model of mature male development. Freedman (1979), however, employed Loevinger's more Piagetian model in his description of faculty development (see figure 3). He suggests in the first of five stages that faculty members assume a simplistic view of their role in the institution and focus primarily on their own discipline. Faculty then move to a second stage that leads to increasingly complex views of the world (a stage that is common to all Piagetian models). Some faculty may never move to this second stage, though most do.

A smaller number of faculty, according to Freedman, reach the third, fourth, or fifth stages. Freedman's fourth stage offers great freedom for faculty in their appreciation of alternative modes of thought and action and in their openness to serve in the role of both teacher and learner. Faculty often enter this fourth stage in their senior years. As Stephen Abbot and other faculty members like him begin to recognize that new learning comes in many different forms and at many unanticipated times in their lives, so will learning for students come in ways that can be neither anticipated nor controlled. Students must find their own answers. Faculty must do no more (or less) than create conditions to maximize this potential for learning.

The fifth and final stage, according to Freedman, embraces a classic Piagetian emphasis on individual and autonomous conceptualization. Faculty begin to build their own distinctive philosophy of education and become teachers and mentors to other faculty. They readily embrace contradiction, complexity, ambivalence, and change in their own life and in the classroom. They become educational leaders of their institutions through example if not through formal actions and influence. Stephen Abbot seems to be on the edge of this stage, though, without institutional support, he may never realize the opportunity to make much use of his own perspectives (other than through participation in this case study analysis).

Freedman's model offers a developmental challenge for all collegiate institutions: The institution will be successful to the extent that it can move not only its students, but also its faculty to a more mature level of development. As with other Piagetian models, Freedman's construct is potentially fraught with normative problems. Is the movement to a more complex and abstract state of cognition a sign of intellectual maturation or one of socialization to the dominant (often masculine) emphasis on detachment and objectivity? To what extent is maturation in a Piagetian sense dominated by a psychological emphasis on interpersonal relationships and bias toward integration and interdisciplinarity?

The misapplication of adult development theory to faculty

Adult development theory is not without its detractors, and it must be applied with some reservation in the analysis of faculty needs and the formulation of strategies for faculty revitalization. First, the models of adult development are often filled with biases regarding culture, social class, and gender. The shift from "lower-order" functions that produce concrete and context-specific results to "higher-order" functions that produce abstract and readily generalizable results may represent not so much an improvement as the embracing of a specific way of knowing that is often associated with a masculine and northern European American epistemology. A more feminine epistemology (Belenky et al. 1986; Gilligan 1982) emphasizes concrete and context-specific results, as do the epistemologies of many other cultures in the world. Are these latter epistemologies somehow inferior to those of the epistemology offered by males (and some females) in northern Europe and North America, or are they simply not dominant at the present time?

Similarly, the emphasis in Eriksonian models on a prescribed and seemingly invariant progression through certain life phases and stages may present a perspective on normative development that is decidedly Euro-American, masculine, and social/psychological in aspect. This type of progression can become self-fulfilling if viewed uncritically (Mann 1987). If we expect a midlife crisis and consider those of middle age without such a crisis to be either in denial or somehow abnormal, then we are likely to find many people with midlife crises. If we saturate our colleges and universities with programs for the transition to the 50s, then we are likely to find these transitions and the problems associated with them at every turn. When all we have is a hammer, then we will soon begin to see and treat everything else as a nail.

Another concern centers on the apparent universality of many models of adult development. First of all, psychologists do not hold an exclusive claim on them. Sociologists, biologists, and novelists may offer quite different interpretations of changes in life stages. Lower-middle-class men and women may experience quite different midlife crises from those of the upper-middle class (Breneman 1993; Rubin 1976). Asian Americans, African Americans, and Hispanic Americans may engage in significantly different developmental challenges from northern European Americans. People with disabilities and the many people in our world who have experienced major intrusive life events may find the normative stage theories inappropriate.

Even men and women from the same socioeconomic and ethnic backgrounds may go through different stages as a result of having been born in a different era. Sheehy (1995, p. 4) suggests that all of Erikson's and Levinson's stages of adult development may now occur 10 years later. Baby boomers may be going through midlife transitions 10 years later than people born before World War II. For boomers, 50 "is now what 40 used to be. Sixty is what 50 used to be" (p. 4). Adult development theory may be misapplied to faculty development programs precisely because of these potential differences and because the population of faculty in our colleges and universities is becoming increasingly diverse (Mann 1987). Greater breadth is needed in the study of development among faculty—and among all adults for that matter—who are not northern European American males.

> *The various theories of adult development are very useful in illuminating different stages, phases, individual differences, or critical events in the lives of faculty members [that] are likely to have an impact on faculty career growth and development, and ultimately on faculty vitality. However, it is also important to understand that one theory of adult development is probably not sufficient for a full understanding of faculty lives. Although some faculty may have lives [that] follow the patterns outlined by Hodgkinson or Levinson, . . . others*

> *may follow patterns [that] are not age related. It is not*
> *safe for faculty developers to assume, for instance, that*
> *all faculty who are age 55 or older are interested in*
> *retirement-planning workshops* (D. Kelly 1991, p. 11).

One's stage of adult development certainly plays a major role in determining the level of interest in and commitment to certain forms of productivity, but other factors also play a significant role. The next paragraphs examine nine of them.

Socialization

In studies of faculty, level of academic socialization is the fundamental and most powerful predictor of research productivity (Wheeler and Creswell 1985). A study of two faculty groups at a large research university matched, in terms of generation, rank, and age, 63 faculty who were "highly active" in teaching, research, and service with 66 randomly selected tenured faculty (Corcoran and Clark 1984). The two groups differed significantly with regard to socialization. When asked what they found satisfying about work, the first group consistently reported academic freedom and the ability to contribute through research, but the "representative group" did not consistently list these factors as top aspects of work.

Thus, the importance of professional values in productivity should not be underestimated. In highly developed professions, these values undergird nearly every action. For example, how a physician makes decisions with and interacts with patients is guided by powerful values well inculcated through years of medical school and training. Similarly, an effective attorney or clergyman or -woman knows more than the law or religion. They have learned many unwritten rules, concepts, values, and behaviors that allow them to "act like an attorney" or "think like a priest," and these competencies facilitate their work. Given that this feature is fundamental in a productive faculty member, strategies that capitalize on these values are likely to increase productivity. Conversely, one should be careful in making changes that undermine these highly socialized processes, values, or practices.

Motivation

Studies of scientists have found that internal motivation plays a pivotal role in productivity (Pelz and Andrews 1966). Regardless of their stage in life, the scientists in these studies who were driven in their work by a personal desire were more productive. Further, the development of strong inner motivation was important in assuring productivity over a life span. Older scientists who maintained their productivity also had maintained their high level of motivation (Pelz and Andrews 1966). Fortunately, most senior faculty today remain enthusiastic about their work. A survey of 1,135 senior faculty at six institutions of higher education found they "remain internally controlled, vital, and productive while being active in areas of teaching, scholarship, and service. . . . Senior faculty [do] not want to give up their jobs and . . . would choose an academic career if they could make the decision again" (Armour et al. 1990, abstract). Moreover, senior faculty are likely to report more satisfaction in their careers than younger faculty, although some evidence suggests that the transition points in the careers of senior faculty can lead to decreased satisfaction (Baldwin 1990).

Thus, "motivation" is not determined solely by internal factors but by an interaction between the faculty member's own shifting needs and interests and the characteristics of the environment in which he or she works, as is the case with Stephen Abbot. The level of satisfaction with one's job and one's willingness to work hard depends in part—perhaps in large part—on one's perception of self in relationship to the work environment (Super 1957). If an academic environment reinforces a notion of personal competence and effectiveness, then a senior faculty member is likely to be enthusiastic, and feel competent, in his or her work—regardless of age and the potential decline in mental abilities.

The theory of expectancy provides some insight as to how these external factors contribute to motivation (Lawrence and Blackburn 1988; Vroom 1964). To oversimplify, this theory suggests that people are motivated to an action, in this case to stay current and be productive, when they believe that the effort they expend on updating their knowledge will actually bring them up to speed, that being more up to date will result in positive outcomes, and that the positive outcomes available for being up to date and productive are ones they value (Farr and Middlebrooks 1990). Applying this theory to faculty development helps to explain why many traditional efforts at faculty development fail. For example, making sabbaticals, continuing education, and fellowships more available may provide faculty members a means to update their abilities, but seldom do these activities have positive outcomes, beyond personal satisfaction, for participating in them. Fortunately, this missing aspect of most efforts at faculty development could be easy to correct. Effective faculty rewards are well known, not expensive, and fairly easy to provide. The theory of expectancy suggests that providing these valued rewards for faculty who participate in updating their behavior and who are productive would increase participation in these activities.

Content Knowledge and Skills (Research, Artistic, Teaching, and Service)

To be a highly effective faculty member, one must, without question, be up to date and knowledgeable about one's content area and about the relevant current teaching, research, service, and, if appropriate, artistic skills.

As discussed earlier, studies have found that age is not the major predictor of being less current in one's field. In fact, with regard to intellectual ability, currency, and motivation, no reason exists to expect less because of age. Rather, we can expect similar, perhaps more sophisticated, cognitive productivity from older faculty members.

Prevention is the best strategy for ensuring the ongoing competence of senior faculty members.

Still, there is no question that it is becoming increasingly difficult for *all* faculty to stay abreast of the exploding amount of knowledge and the enormous continual changes in technology. In a matter of years, one can, at any age, be quickly left behind in his or her field. Thus, this area is of concern for the continued vitality of faculty of all ages. It appears important to maintain a sense of momentum and continual growth among faculty members to avoid having to develop programs later to deal with disconnected, out-of-date, burned-out faculty. This theme (one to which we will return later) emerges frequently throughout the literature: Prevention is the best strategy for ensuring the ongoing competence of senior faculty members.

Vital Network-Professional Communication

Effective academic work requires frequent and meaningful contact among colleagues. Although much faculty work is done alone or in small teams, faculty need constant contact with other productive faculty (both inside and outside their institutions) to keep current and to test ideas and strategies for research or teaching. Faculty members' productivity and effectiveness are increased through formal interaction with colleagues, such as peer review of articles and grants, and through informal interaction, such as e-mail, phone calls, and conversations in the hall. A vital network of colleagues is so important that it is consistently found to be a major predictor of productivity in research (Blackburn 1979; Bland and Schmitz 1986; Pelz and Andrews 1966). Faculty members' productivity may shift over time, not as a function of age but as a function of the amount of time a senior faculty member spends with colleagues. Further, some senior faculty may become less productive because of the tendency of people after age 50 to reduce the size of their network of friends and colleagues (Bergquist, Greenburg, and Klaum 1993).

In the study of faculty at a Midwest research university noted earlier, the highly productive faculty had much more active and professionally meaningful relationships with colleagues than less productive faculty (Corcoran and Clark 1984). Another study, of 10,000 scientists in 1,200 different research groups in six countries, similarly found that the most productive researchers had the most frequent conversations with colleagues and spent the most time doing such things as reviewing drafts of colleagues' papers, visiting each others' labs, and exchanging reprints (Pelz and Andrews 1966).

A survey of 42 Lilly fellows at a large public research institution found "the most common method of handling both teaching and research problems, at all faculty levels, was to discuss the matter with one's colleagues" (Kalivoda, Sorrell, and Simpson 1994, p. 265). Colleagues in one's network provide advice about how to resolve classroom problems, what courses to develop, and what teaching strategies to use (Finkelstein 1982). And a review of academic networks concludes that "clear and substantial evidence [exists] that faculty who communicate more with colleagues produce more and better research [and have] quicker promotion, increased income, higher frequency of distinguished awards, [and] higher satisfaction with the work itself" (Hitchcock, Bland, Hekelman, and Blumenthal 1995, p. 1112). In short, ensuring mechanisms for frequent communication with productive colleagues is important to the vitality of faculty and may be particularly important for senior faculty, who at this point in their lives often are inclined to retreat from extensive interpersonal relationships (Bergquist, Greenburg, and Klaum 1993).

Simultaneous Projects

Several researchers have similarly found that having multiple, simultaneous projects under way is associated with productivity for established faculty (Hargens 1978; Stinchcombe 1966). Such an arrangement seems to provide continuous stimulation and a buffer against disillusionment or feeling stuck; if an important project fails, stalls, or proves unsuccessful, another is already up and running. Stephen Abbot added the interdisciplinary study of postmodernism to his ongoing interest in literature. Perhaps it contributes to his own ongoing vitality.

Work Time

Faculty have always put in more time than the standard 40-hour work week. The question is how much time and what distribution of time across tasks is necessary to be productive in the areas of importance to oneself and to the institution. If an institution wants faculty members to be highly productive in research, according to a study of publication rates of scientists in university and industry settings, less than 10 percent of one's time allotted to research is insufficient, and 40 percent is probably ideal (Knorr, Mittermeir, Aichholzer, and Waller 1979). Others advise that a commitment of at least 50 percent of one's time is necessary to be successful in research.

The optimal time commitment needed for effective teaching is less clear; however, in 1991, a summary of national surveys of faculty found that both senior and nonsenior faculty at four-year institutions typically teach classes nine hours or more a week and that 23 percent teach classes for 13 hours or more (El-Khawas 1991). At two-year institutions, most faculty teach classes at least nine hours each week and 78 percent report over 13 hours of in-class time each week. If one estimates two to three hours of outside class time per each hour in class for preparation, grading, and advising, the total becomes considerable. For faculty needing to also succeed in research, an additional commitment of 40 percent of one's time is necessary, which does not include the time most faculty invest in institutional and professional service and outreach. It is no wonder that half the faculty are not satisfied with their teaching load or with their opportunities (or lack thereof) for scholarly pursuits (El-Khawas 1991).

Unfortunately, it is becoming increasingly difficult for faculty to devote sufficient time to the primary tasks of teaching, research, service, and outreach. As state funding for faculty work has decreased and competition for federal research funds become keener, many faculty spend more time on activities aimed at generating income than on those associated directly with teaching and research. For example, many faculty at research universities report that the number of federal grant applications that must be written has significantly increased so that research can be funded. Faculty spend more time in staff and janitorial work as shortfalls are managed by reducing staff. In the health sciences, enormous changes in the health-care system have resulted in faculty members' spending increasingly more time in patient care to generate needed income—taking away time that was formerly spent on teaching and research (Bland and Holloway 1995).

Orientation

Early research suggested that prolific researchers were predominately externally oriented rather than oriented toward their institutions. More recent work, however, finds that these faculty are both externally and internally oriented. While they are highly active in external institutional activities such as disciplinary societies and conferences, they are not less involved internally (Blackburn and Lawrence 1986; Finkelstein 1984). "Highly active" faculty are heavily involved with major decisions on campus (such as governance and redesign of curricula) as well as involved outside the institution (Corcoran and Clark 1984). These results suggest that productive instructors are also both externally and internally oriented.

Autonomy and Commitment

Autonomy and independence are highly valued aspects of academic life. Based on three national studies, "more than eight in 10 senior faculty . . . [are] satisfied with their autonomy and independence" (El-Khawas 1991, p. 7). Older faculty seem to enjoy working alone and appreciate the independence that their status as senior (and usually tenured) professors affords them. Yet among community college faculty from the humanities and social sciences in Virginia who have served their institutions or systems over 20 years, the primary source of satisfaction was not their autonomy but their connectedness (Tucker 1990). "Even when other levels of faculty satisfaction began to wane, community college faculty still believed in the goals and ideals of community-driven education. Even when the institution or the administration disappointed them, they never doubted their choice of profession or the importance of their mission" (Tucker 1990, p. 10). Being committed to one's institution is not unique to community college faculty. An intensive study of 18 senior professors at a major research university reveals that faculty at this stage in their careers similarly find particular satisfaction in "being part of the academic community" (Braskamp et al. 1982, p. 14).

Several authors in business and higher education have noted this "tight-loose" arrangement between an organization and its productive, seasoned members (Cole and Cole 1967; Peters and Waterman 1988). For example, studies on commitment to and involvement in work reveal that workers who keep climbing the professional ladder maintain a higher level of commitment to work than those who do not (Baldwin 1990; Kanter 1979; Patton 1978; Schuster and Wheeler 1990).

> *Faculty who conceive of themselves as among the "moving" rather than the "stuck" will be likely to keep their aspirations high, have positive self-esteem, work hard, take appropriate risks, remain engaged in their interests, remain involved with their students and colleagues, and advocate constructive organizational change* (Votruba 1990, p. 218).

The most productive faculty are those who have the freedom to choose their own research and to plan their activities and time but who also believe they are valued by and an important part of the governance and success of their institutions.

The tie between productivity and commitment has also been highlighted in the corporate literature (see, e.g., Reichheld 1996). A study that compared thriving companies with those that have failed in our turbulent times found that:

> *. . . the companies with the highest [employee] retention rate earned the best profits. Relative retention explains*

*profit better than market share, scale, cost position, or
any of the other variables usually associated with competitive advantage. It also explains why traditional
management techniques [such as downsizing] often
backfire in chaotic ways* (Reichheld 1996, p. 23).

"Business loyalty has three dimensions—customer loyalty,
employee loyalty, and investor loyalty—and . . . they are far
more powerful, far-reaching, and interdependent than we
had anticipated or imagined" (Reichheld 1996, p. 3). The
linchpin of these three factors, however, is employee loyalty.
Without employee loyalty it is not possible to maintain a
loyal customer base (in our case, student base) or investor
base (in our case, donors and funders), which is why so
many management experts argue that continuous employment is the key to creativity, productivity, and organizational
"nimbleness." In short, it behooves higher education institutions to maintain commitment and loyalty in faculty.

Morale

Morale is included here as an internal factor, although one's
morale is primarily affected by institutional factors. High
morale is a desired quality for faculty because it is associated
with greater investment in work. "Morale is based on such
factors as . . . leadership, and a sense of shared purpose
with and loyalty to others in the organization" (Austin and
Gamson 1983, p. 43). The most frequent sources of high
morale include stimulating colleagues, autonomy (freedom
to choose one's own research and plan one's time, for example), an administration that is appreciative and supportive,
peer support, trust of administration, satisfactory work conditions, level of compensation, and few self-perceptions of
being "stuck" (Eckert and Stecklein 1961; McKeachie 1982).

In general, faculty morale has varied over time and by type
of institution. It declined in the 1970s and 1980s. For example,
a study of 5,000 faculty found 40 percent who said they were
less enthusiastic than previously and 33 percent who said
they were interested in considering another profession (Carnegie Foundation 1985); the same survey in the late 1980s
found modest improvement in morale (Carnegie Foundation
1989). But a national survey of 392 colleges and universities
across the country in 1989 found that senior faculty do not
appear to be burned out (El-Khawas 1991). Moreover, senior

faculty in general are usually not planning to retire early. Rather, they still plan to retire at 65 and want to remain active and participate in some professional capacity after retirement. Thus, there is no reason to expect senior faculty to be less excited about their work than are their younger colleagues; in fact, they may be more enthusiastic (El-Khawas 1991).

Conclusions

So far this monograph has discussed the intrinsic factors that influence senior faculty members' abilities to meet the major tasks confronting higher education. There is no reason to expect their mental abilities, motivation, content knowledge, technical skills, or morale to decline because of age. And there is no reason to expect less productivity and creativity from faculty because of the stage of their careers or development. In many ways, age and experience provide the benefits of rich, highly integrated cognitive structures and interest in broader and interdisciplinary issues, a desire to facilitate others' success, and a need to focus energies on productive activities that have enduring meaningful impact.

Senior faculty also bring to bear on issues a deep sense of commitment to their institutions, highly inculcated values, a need to focus on meaningful projects, a vital (often world-wide) network of professional colleagues, knowledge of the academic enterprise (its governance, funding, and decision-making processes), and an ability to manage (even thrive on) multiple, simultaneous projects. Two major themes are apparent in the writings discussed thus far that influence whether a faculty member will or will not emerge in the senior years with these positive characteristics: (1) the interplay between individual and institutional factors, and (2) preventing "stuckness" and maintaining momentum and competence. We will return to these themes in the final sections on promoting faculty vitality. The following section, however, examines the extrinsic factors that affect the productivity and vitality of senior faculty.

LOOKING OUTSIDE FOR VITALITY:
Institutional Factors Affecting the Productivity of Senior Faculty

The changing experiences of Stephen Abbot resulted not only from his own personal maturation, but also from the profound changes that were taking place in his institution. Shifts in public funding, changes in students' interests and values, and the politics of his university and state all contributed to the changing character of the vitality that Stephen Abbot brought to his career. While it is essential for their productivity that faculty members possess the individual characteristics listed in figure 1, those characteristics are insufficient. Of all the factors that affect a researcher's productivity, none are as powerful as the environmental features of the workplace (Clark and Lewis 1985). In higher education, in particular:

> . . . place of employment is the single best predictor of faculty scholarly productivity. . . . Faculty [members] who come to productive surroundings produce more there than they did before they arrived and more than they will later if they move to a less productive environment. Resources, support, challenge, communication with producers on other campuses, all correlate with a professor's productivity (Pellino et al. 1981, p. 15).

Of all the factors that affect a researcher's productivity, none are as powerful as the environmental features of the workplace.

Other studies have similarly revealed that institutional features are the most powerful predictors of productivity in research (see, e.g., Blackburn, Behymer, and Hall 1978; Bland, Hitchcock, Anderson, and Stritter 1987; Clark and Lewis 1985; Long and McGinnis 1981; McGee and Ford 1987; Perkoff 1986). Perhaps the most convincing of these studies followed faculty as they moved from one institution to another; they found that a faculty member's research productivity changes, depending on the institution. These changes were not primarily a function of the individual or of the internal factors described in the previous section.

This finding was true even for faculty members who produced the most research. When relocated to an institution that was less oriented toward research, their productivity decreased (Long and McGinnis 1981), which perhaps explains why the strategy of hiring one "research star" to bring up a group's research productivity seldom works. Given the important interplay of institutional and individual features in vitality, this finding is not surprising. A faculty member's productivity is greatly affected by his or her surroundings: the quality of students, the productivity of colleagues, the availability of resources, the culture and climate, the administrative structure and decision-making processes. Faculty work is a very social enterprise, depending a great deal on interactions that are facilitated—or not—by one's environment (Fox 1991).

What are the features of Stephen Abbot's institution that facilitated his professional vitality, and what are the features that dampened his enthusiasm? What are the features of any collegiate institution that facilitate or impede faculty vitality and productivity? The most frequent measure of faculty productivity is research. So, while it is only one aspect of a faculty member's role, these studies do provide a profile of institutions in which faculty excel in this area that matches with the fewer studies that looked at other measures of outcome.

A comprehensive review of productive research organizations found a consistent set of features in these institutions (Bland and Ruffin 1992): clear goals that serve a coordinating function; an emphasis on the institution's priorities; the academic culture; a positive climate; assertive participative governance; decentralized organization; frequent communication; sufficient and accessible resources; a critical mass of faculty who have been together for a while and bring different perspectives to the mix (the size, age, and diversity of the group); adequate and fair salaries and other rewards; targeted recruitment and selection; a brokered opportunity structure; and seasoned, participative academic leadership (see figure 1). Although these factors are discussed separately, the reader should keep in mind that they operate as an interdependent whole. Together they provide the environment that is most conducive to faculty and institutional vitality.

To set the stage for the consideration of these factors, we begin with an examination of the forces that integrate a faculty member's personal aspirations and goals with the organizational environment in which the faculty member operates. These forces concern a faculty member's career and, more specifically, the *stage* of a career in which a faculty member is operating when experiencing the highly influential organizational factors identified (Bland and Ruffin 1992).

Career Development
In the past, faculty members were typically hired for full-time positions during their 20s immediately upon (or even before) completing an advanced degree or advanced voca-

tional training. As a result, these young men and women avoided a developmental challenge encountered by virtually everyone else in a modern western society: They did not have to adjust to an entirely different institution. These traditional faculty members have spent essentially their entire lives in educational institutions. They entered school at age 5 and have remained in some type of educational institution for the remainder of their active adult lives (Bergquist 1993a; Furniss 1981). Unlike other people in our society, who must successfully negotiate at least one major transition—between an educational institution and some other institution (business, military, domestic, for example)—many faculty members have never known a different world and have never had to make a major career change or even a change in the type of institution with which they are affiliated. As a result, traditional faculty at midcareer are more likely than other professionals and other mature members of our society to view the prospects of shifting careers and leaving education as very daunting and become quite anxious about entering a new job market for the first time in their lives. Because traditional faculty members often have not had to face the many career transitions and challenges that lie at the heart of most career development models (Bergquist 1993a), these models must be adjusted for these men and women.

Conversely, nontraditional faculty members who have done something else before becoming educators—who enter a collegiate institution as gifted tradespeople or seasoned professionals—are more likely to view the prospects of returning to the real world of noneducational institutions as perhaps disappointing but certainly not profoundly upsetting. In many instances, these nontraditional faculty members have taken a cut in pay to become faculty members or left high-status or secure jobs to become members of a collegiate faculty. These faculty members are often more open than their more traditional colleagues to educational experimentation, to various part-time employment opportunities, and to reorganization plans, precisely because of their previous experience in other careers (Bergquist 1993a).

The world is clearly changing for most faculty members—as well as many other members of our society. The conventional conception of career as one life/one career is no longer viable for most professionals (Sarason 1977). At least two shifts in career during one's life will be common—even for faculty. While a senior faculty member who is deeply embedded in an institution may never be required to shift careers, he or she may be given the option of changing careers or may at least wish to shift emphases within his or her own career as a way of getting "unstuck" from boring or frustrating work. Thus, the newly emerging models of career development are particularly relevant to the formulation of strategies for the revitalization of senior faculty (as well as the continuing vitality of younger faculty).

Independent career development models

Some of the models of career development are extensions of adult development theory; others have been derived independently. We begin with the best known independently derived model—Holland's theory of vocational preferences (1985). This model of career development is based on the assumption that we tend to select and remain in specific vocations based on an interaction between our enduring personality traits and specific characteristics of the environment. Holland identified six primary personality traits (realistic, investigative, artistic, social, enterprising, and conventional) and six comparable environments, and suggests that vocational satisfaction is based at least in part on a match between type and environment.

Unlike most authors in the field, whose theories of satisfaction in one's career are based on adult development, Holland assumes that vocational types are relatively stable over time and that, as a result, satisfaction with a career is also likely to be relatively stable over time, provided the environment does not change. Thus, a faculty member who prefers a realistic vocation is likely to thrive as a teacher of technology or crafts, whereas a faculty member who is investigative will find comfort in the sciences, a faculty member with artistic preferences will continue to thrive in the arts and humanities, and a faculty member with strong social needs will be gratified by teaching, counseling, and committee work that enables him or her to understand, help, teach, or lead other people.

While Holland's typology has proved of great value to many career counselors and job recruiters, it does not adequately address the complex dynamics of shifting career paths—and in particular the atypical conflicts associated with the careers of faculty members in contemporary colleges and universities. Holland's model fails to fully incorporate influential factors that lie outside the realm of the environment in which a person works—including his or her own shifting internal needs and processes of maturation. Stephen Abbot, for instance, may have been initially attracted to the humanities because of an artistic preference, but at various phases in his career, Abbot was much more interested in students as learners than in teaching the content of his discipline, suggesting a preference for social relationships.

Another model (Super 1957) is perhaps more applicable to the careers of faculty. Super's model emphasizes changes in an individual's self-concept rather than the completion of specific life tasks. Super believes that one's choice of career does not end with an initial job choice but is a continuous process involving shifts in self-perception throughout life. The key factor leading to vocational success is not the good match between personality and environment that Holland suggests but the ability to adjust one's sense of self in response to the various experiences one has in a specific occupation. Super believes that maturation and stages of adult development, on the one hand, and career development, on the other hand, are closely related: "Career-related behavior is affected by the demands of one's life cycle. As a person matures, progress occurs through a series of developmental career life stages, with opportunities at each stage to successfully encounter specific tasks" (Pietrofesa and Splete 1996, p. 141). Yet Super does not rely heavily on adult development theory, focusing instead on the specific ways in which we perceive and interpret job-related experiences at various points in our lives.

During the senior years, career interests tend to decline and, in many cases, become static (Super et al. 1963). Our sense of self at this later point in life is often tied, not to our careers, but to other aspects of our lives. Moreover, Super suggests, our physical and mental energy begin to decline and we are asked to play new roles, often with less visibility or power than was formerly the case. Thus, at the final stage of a career, one disengages from his or her commitment to a career and begins to invest energy in other areas of life.

While the assumption in most traditional (premodern) and modern societies is that adults will remain in a single career throughout their lives, the emerging concept of multiple careers is supported and documented by Super. His model not only embraces the notion of continual change and vocational adjustments, but also acknowledges the importance of continuity between careers, given that one's second or third career usually bears some resemblance to the first career if one has had a successful life (Wrightsman 1988, pp. 152, 163).

While the multicareer/multistage models, such as Super offers, are responsive to our recognition of shifting priorities, particularly in a changing and turbulent world, they often fail to acknowledge the full diversity of careers in our society. Some men and women will continue to have single careers, while others are likely to have complex careers that are not easily described by any unified model. It is likely that the very pattern of the career varies from person to person. While Super acknowledged that several different career patterns exist, he could not have anticipated the dramatic differences that would emerge during these last decades of the 20th century (Driver 1979, 1982).

Career development models based on adult development models

Many theories of adult development—especially those that apply general adult development theory to students or faculty members and their careers in American colleges and universities—focus primarily on career. Havighurst (1964), for instance, offers a six-stage theory of vocational development that includes identification with a worker (ages 5–10), acquiring the basic habits of industry (10–15), acquiring identity as a worker in the occupational structure (15–25), becoming a productive person (25–40), maintaining a productive society (40–70), and contemplating a productive and responsible life (70 and older) (p. 216). Corresponding in many ways to Erikson's stage of generativity, Havighurst's fifth stage concerns broadening one's concerns beyond individual achievement to a productive society. A man or women at this fifth stage focuses on civic responsibility associated with his or her job, often serves in the role of leader, being at the peak of his or her career, and works closely with younger people in their successful achievement of the third and fourth stages.

While Havighurst's theory benefits from his focus on experiences over a lifetime, he fails—as do most other adult development theorists—to give sufficient attention to the variable of age and to such confounding variables as degree of success in one's career, rank and position in the institution, and significant achievements (such as tenure and major publications in the case of faculty). Independent career development theorists such as Holland, in contrast, tend to focus too much on these latter variables, often categorizing people not in terms of their age, but in terms of their occupation, rank, or institutional role.

Applying career development models to faculty

The independent career development models, such as Super's stages, may be more applicable to faculty careers than are career models based on adult development theory. A "reconceptualized" model of career development, for instance, emphasizes multiple stages and multiple careers (Wheeler and Schuster 1990), encouraging faculty to take advantage of opportunities within the institution or within their own discipline that enable them to make new use of existing skills or to develop skills that they have not yet mastered.

For example, faculty at the State University of New York are more likely to seek out opportunities for retraining and respecialization if they are an associate or full professor than if they are at a lower rank (Finkelstein 1984). This study reinforces the emerging assumption that people wish to shift careers—or at least certain aspects of their careers—as they enter midlife. In fact, we may find that multiple careers are even more common among faculty in the 1990s than they were during the early 1980s.

While the multiple-career models may be appropriate in understanding many aspects of faculty revitalization, faculty careers can also be understood in terms of adult development theory. Many contemporary faculty members may not be seeking a major shift in careers. They may, like Stephen Abbot, want to move in new directions in their current careers. Faculty in midlife could have more diverse and even contradictory needs regarding their careers than has been assumed among those who conceive of faculty as leading stable and uncomplicated lives of contemplative and tenured security. For instance, the needs of midcareer faculty are fairly diverse and complex, partly because faculty members are confronted with both personal and professional challenges, like most middle-class men and women in their 50s (Simpson and Jackson 1990; see also Bergquist, Greenburg, and Klaum 1993).

Many midcareer faculty have attained their professional goals and are now perceiving their careers in new ways (Simpson and Jackson 1990). They want to use new teaching methods and/or teach different subject matter. They are more interested in collaborative, cross-disciplinary activities than earlier in their careers (Lawrence 1985), often wish to expand and diversify roles in their institutions (Baldwin 1979), and seem to be increasingly interested in teaching and becoming institutional leaders, often at the expense of research (Baldwin 1979).

The model of male development offered by Levinson and his colleagues seems to be particularly popular in seeking to understand the shifting career needs of many faculty members (Levinson, Darrow, Klein, Levinson, and McKee 1976). A widely cited five-stage model of faculty career development derived specifically from Levinson's model was recently revised to four stages (see figure 3 on p. 45): novice professor (getting into the academic world), early academic career (settling down and making a name), midcareer (accepting a career plateau or setting new goals), and late career (leaving a legacy) (Baldwin 1979, 1990).

During their senior years, faculty . . . are likely to become more diversified in their interests and activities, perhaps listening and responding to "voices from other rooms."

Like Erikson, Levinson, and multistage-career theorists such as Super, Baldwin suggests that faculty move through periods of relative stability and other periods of stressful change and transition. He also suggests, like Super, that continuity exists over the span of one's career, given that one continues to serve as an academic professional and to perform essentially the same duties: teaching, research and scholarship, and service. The highest level of satisfaction with one's career, according to Baldwin, is found at the final stage, with a growing level of satisfaction to be found at both the third stage and (provided a faculty member is able to find new and more personally based career goals) the fifth stage. During their senior years (stages four and five), faculty often assume administrative duties, shift research interests, or become increasingly active in professional organizations. They are likely to become more diversified in their interests and activities, perhaps listening and responding to "voices from other rooms" (Bergquist, Greenburg, and Klaum 1993), and will "continue to grow well beyond the time they surmount the final, formal academic hurdle—full professorship" (Baldwin and Blackburn 1981, p. 607).

Midcareer adults have often confronted their dreams for a career and found that they have been fulfilled, have not been fulfilled, or are not as satisfying as originally anticipated even when they are fulfilled (Levinson 1996; Levinson et al. 1978). New dreams often supersede the old dreams of our 20s. Men and women who have been devoted to a career throughout their adult lives are inclined to formulate a new dream during their late 40s or early 50s that embraces family and community involvement as well as personal (even idiosyncratic) interests. These new dreams move beyond traditional individual achievement in one's discipline or institution. This concept of the new dream seems quite appropriate for many midcareer faculty who have formulated new dreams and found new niches in their institutions to meet emerging personal interests and needs.

This niche may be found in many different parts of the institution. As reported by a study of midcareer faculty in the humanities at a large urban university, the niche may be an honors program that serves as a vehicle for emerging interdisciplinary interests or foreign travel that not only enhances their teaching, but also meets the emerging need for midlife adventure (Caffarella, Armour, Fuhrmann, and Wergin 1989). Midcareer dreams also offer an opportunity for faculty to exhibit their generative tendencies (Bergquist, Greenburg, and Klaum 1993). Many midcareer faculty want to leave a legacy in their discipline or at an institution (Baldwin 1984), knowing that they have made a difference. But other faculty at midcareer are inclined to live lives of stagnation rather than generativity. They become disengaged from their discipline or institution, and their historical perspective becomes stifling ("we've already tried that") rather than liberating.

While Baldwin's focus was specifically on male faculty in liberal arts colleges, his model has been broadly applied, which may be inappropriate given the different developmental stages for many women and minorities, as well as the different career paths for faculty in other kinds of institutions. It is increasingly difficult to assign faculty to specific stages or to predict exactly what the problems are likely to be that they will encounter at each stage of a career (Baldwin 1990).

Another author also uses Levinson's model as the basis for a three-stage model of faculty careers (see figure 3 on p.

45) (Furniss 1981). Early career focuses on such tasks as finding a mentor, achieving tenure, and settling down in one's career. The second stage, midcareer, focuses on gaining autonomy (a goal that is usually more important for faculty and other professionals than for the general population), becoming mentors, and broadening one's range of interests. At the third and final stage, late career, faculty continue to broaden their range of interests, become less competitive (at least among males), and assume a role of leadership that calls for experience and wisdom.

Furniss, like many other career development theorists, declares that his model is not related to age: "Entry on a faculty career is most common for the young, but it is also possible for the middle-aged or . . . the old" (Furniss 1981, p. 84). While Furniss offers valuable insights about career development, particularly in his case studies of seven faculty at various stages of their academic careers, he repeats the problem encountered by many career development theorists, focusing too much attention on financial and job-related issues without giving adequate consideration to the relationship between these issues and other more personal and interpersonal aspects of a faculty member's life.

The misapplication of career development theory to faculty

Just as adult development theory has certain limitations when applied to any specific population—and in particular faculty—so must we be cautious in the application of career development models to faculty. As several adult and career development theorists and researchers have noted, adults in their 50s and 60s are likely to move in increasingly diverse ways, making generalizations inappropriate. What does seem to hold true for most senior faculty members, however, is the theme of potential or actual vitality—and the need for this vitality to be understood and appreciated by other people.

Most senior faculty view the issue of continuing service to their institutions as critical, provided they are given "meaningful work that is recognized and respected by others" (Baldwin 1990, p. 37). These members of the faculty realize that they still have many years left at the college or university, especially if they do not take early retirement and perhaps even choose to remain employed after age 65. Mentoring programs and special projects can be very gratifying (but must be optional) for senior faculty, and they can often rejuvenate the careers of senior faculty. They are essential if these faculty members are to remain committed to the institution and be productive during the last third of their academic careers.

The discussion in the remainder of this section focuses on those organizational and institutional factors that directly influence productivity and vitality (see figure 1 on p. 40).

Clear Goals That Serve a Coordinating Function

Productive organizations, corporate or educational, consistently set clear goals for their employees to strive toward. A review of 20 years of research on faculty and institutional vitality, for example, found that vital institutions are characterized by clear, coordinating goals (Bland and Schmitz 1988). This finding does not mean that faculty work is narrowly directed, for autonomy is an important individual characteristic of the productive researcher. But a classic study of 10,000 scientists in 1,200 organizations in six countries found that individual autonomy is compatible with goals for the group (Pelz and Andrews 1966). A Bell Labs researcher said, "Everyone must know what the overall goal is so that within each [person's] area, he [or she] can look for those solutions that are most relevant to the major goals." Added another, "The organization points out what mountain they want us to climb, but how we climb it is up to us."

The right mix of and balance between coordination and autonomy are important. Stephen Abbot, for instance, would have benefited from both greater clarity, coherence, and consistency in the goals of his university and greater assurance of autonomy in his work as a faculty member, but the volatility of California politics has probably made either clear goals or sustained autonomy impossible. Studies that have looked at the balance between coordination and autonomy find that, in general, performance is low when no coordination exists or, conversely, when an effort is made to completely control the direction of academics' work (Katz 1978; Pelz and Andrews 1966; Pineau and Levy-Leboyer 1983). In the most loosely coordinated groups, for example, only the most motivated researchers excel (Pelz and Andrews 1966).

A middle ground that balances coordination and autonomy is clearly most conducive to productivity. Organizational goals are clear and agreed upon, but each individual has significant autonomy in deciding how to contribute to the goals' achievement. Getting consensus on overall goals and keeping the priority ones in people's minds is challenging at any level above the small work group. Thus, it is easy to see how many of the following characteristics are also found in vital organizations: e.g., identifying and emphasizing top-priority goals, frequent communication, participative governance, and aligned rewards.

An Emphasis on the Institution's Priorities

Productive organizations emphasize their top-priority goals in their mission statements, faculty hired, reward systems, organizational structures, and more. In colleges and universities, it can be difficult to emphasize one or two goals over others. But the impact of doing so greatly increases productivity in that area, and the lack of doing so is not neutral, but negative. To be productive in research, the institution must give research the same priority, if not more, than other goals.

For example, institutions that put more weight on research in decisions about promotion and tenure (Bean 1982) or focus more on graduate training and less on undergraduate training show greater productivity in research (Birnbaum 1983; Blackburn, Behymer, and Hall 1978). Similarly, institutions, colleges, or departments that focus on practitioners' training or service are less productive in research (Baird 1986; Barley and Reman 1979; Perkoff 1986)—which is not an argument for all colleges and universities to emphasize research. But it illustrates the power of emphasizing an institution's priorities throughout the organization to best achieve them.

The Institutional Culture

A study of the nation's colleges where faculty have the highest morale found that these colleges share *"distinctive organizational cultures* that are carefully nurtured and built upon" (Rice and Austin 1988, p. 52; see also Rice and Austin 1990). Organizational culture is a "distinctiveness that sets an organization apart from other similar organizations, and it is a distinctiveness that everyone within the organization understands, shares, and values" (Bland and Ruffin 1992, p. 388). A clear culture:

> . . . *ensures that everyone is on the same boat, and they know where the boat is headed. . . . Identity provides the*

*framework for participants to deal with existential issues
of their own worth and meaning in the organization.*
*Because new people join the institution every year and
the institution changes constantly, a strong sense of
identity must be cultivated, tended, and frequently
revised* (Tierney 1987, p. 70).

Corporations similarly have long been aware of the impact
of a strong culture on productivity (Baird 1986; Collins and
Porras 1994).

Culture, however, is not self-sustaining. It requires attention to maintain the core values and to stop the intrusion of
noncore values, and senior faculty play a particularly pivotal
role in maintaining the culture. With many faculty soon to
be reaching retirement at the same time, or the loss of senior
faculty through early retirement packages, institutions risk
losing their stories, legacies, and institutional wisdom—in
short, their culture (Bergquist 1993a). Moreover, the strength
of the management culture (e.g., total quality management,
responsibility-centered management), collective bargaining,
and a legalistic/adversarial culture has increased on many
campuses. All of these cultures have contributed to the environments of colleges and universities. But recently, their
presence and influence have dramatically increased on many
campuses—with a concomitant weakening of the academic
culture.

One 25-year veteran of a large university in the Midwest
put it succinctly, albeit intemperately, in a letter to the editor
of the *Minneapolis Star-Tribune* after experiencing his institution's attempts to incorporate total quality management, then
reengineering, then responsibility-centered management,
and more:

*Over the last five years . . . the university has become a
haven for every form of washed-out corporate spin doc-
tor or interplanetary industrial consultant and the community as a whole has been forced and twisted to adhere
to their bizarre dictates and dreamscapes. There has been
a steady breakdown in the community ever since. . . .
It is now time that the people who understand this community best truly have a chance at its direction and
preservation. . . . The best answers to the university's problems will be found inside the institution and its people.*

Thus, the leaders who can influence the culture of an institution—the senior faculty members—often are deeply embedded in the traditional collegial culture yet face a strong managerial culture populated with administrators who seem to treat the faculty like "hired hands" (Tucker 1990, p. 8; see also Bergquist 1993a). Senior faculty in one study feel "drained and battered by the system" and believe that teaching has taken "a back seat to some magical FTE formula that rules us all" (Tucker 1990, p. 9). As one senior faculty member said, "I am still committed to this democratic experiment, but it's getting harder all the time" (p. 9).

Under such conditions, faculty certainly do not feel either respected or very influential (Tucker 1990), resulting in senior faculty members' abandoning the leadership roles for which they are now so highly qualified. Alternatively, they stay in those roles, digging in and becoming thorns in the side of the administration. These stubborn senior faculty often lead the highly vocal faculty opposition to virtually all administrative initiatives, thus putting themselves at risk of becoming stagnant and stuck in a negative, regressive stance against institutional change and innovation.

A Positive Climate

Certainly, everyone wants to go to work each day to a place that is uplifting and reinforcing. But does this scenario really affect productivity? The answer clearly is "yes" (Andrews 1979; Birnbaum 1983; Katz 1978; Long and McGinnis 1981; Peters and Waterman 1988; Schweitzer 1988; Turney 1974). Andrews (1979) studied climate by looking at such things as the degree to which faculty feel free to offer their ideas, the opportunities to do so, the weight given to them, and the sense of cooperation, and found that productivity was greater for academics who believed this description fit their environment.

A study of 84 randomly selected research projects in 14 U.S. and one Canadian university found the same results (Birnbaum 1983). In projects that reported low turnover among participants, a good relationship between the leader and members of the group, and discussion of disagreements, productivity was higher, which certainly makes sense in light of the importance of having relationships that allow one to benefit from being around productive peers and sharing a culture. Conversely, other faculty frequently said they were disillusioned with the declining sense of community in their colleges and with the deterioration of intellectual climate and "quality of life" (El-Khawas 1991). In another survey, humanities and social science faculty became "disillusioned with the intellectual climate of the institution the longer they [stayed] in the system" (Tucker 1990, p. 6). While the humanities and social science faculty were "buoyed by collegiality among their faculty cohorts and rewarded by close interactions with diverse students," they were dissatisfied in many cases with the "strained and even hostile relationships between faculty and administrators" (p. 7).

Writings on corporate downsizing illustrate the negative impact on productivity when the climate is not positive. A review of the research in this area finds that "surviving" members of downsized companies become less creative and less likely to take risks. Three years after downsizing, these companies are on average less profitable than similar companies in the same environment that did not downsize (Cascio 1993; Cascio and Morris 1996a, 1996b). In short, productivity and creativity are influenced positively by a positive climate. Thus, strategies to address positive climate are important for faculty members' vitality.

Assertive Participative Governance

Shared governance is a deeply held academic belief. One hypothesis in a study of colleges where morale is high was that "a variety of leadership approaches would work, but . . . what was important was managerial competence" (Rice and Austin 1988, p. 54). What the study found is striking: All 10 of the colleges where morale was highest had the same approach to leadership—"leadership that was aggressively participatory in both individual style and organizational structure" (p. 54; see also Rice and Austin 1990). In fact, one of the most frequent findings in the literature on productivity in research (as well as on other faculty outcomes) is the high positive correlation between participative governance and productivity (Andrews 1979; Bagenstos 1988; Brief 1984; Katz 1978; Okrasa 1987; Pelz 1967; Pelz and Andrews 1966; Sindermann 1985; Steiner 1965). On the other hand, "numerous studies [show] a negative association between effectiveness and bureaucratic, rigid decision making [see, e.g., Staw and Cummings 1988], and [a link has been] identified . . . between standardized, formalized decision processes and a vicious cycle of escalating ineffectiveness [see, e.g., Mausch 1985]" (Cameron and Tschirhart 1992, p. 92).

A study of organizational effectiveness also found that participative governance is more effective and suggests that now, more than ever, a "need [exists] for multiple sources of information and multiple perspectives. . . . Ashby's Law of Requisite Variety suggests that environmental complexity must be managed by equal amounts of internal complexity, and participative decision making allows complexity to be built into the decision-making process" (Cameron and Tschirhart 1992, p. 102). Moreover, managers must resist centralizing decisions in times of stress (Cameron and Tschirhart 1992). Thus, changes that decrease the ability of faculty to participate in decision making or that decrease the collaborative nature of decision making will negatively affect the productivity of faculty members.

Decentralized Organization

Another robust finding in the literature on research productivity is that conducive institutional environments have decentralized structures (Bean 1982; Creswell and Bean 1996; Epson, Payne, and Pearson 1983; Okrasa 1987; Steiner 1965)—which does not mean chaotic. As discussed earlier in this section, the organizational features of productive institutional environments do not work in isolation. A decentralized organization works only in the context of clear, coordinating goals, a common culture, socialized members, a positive climate, frequent communication, and participative governance.

Communication

Communication among local faculty and national faculty, and between faculty and administrators is essential to productivity. And the emergence of the electronic superhighway has significantly increased faculty members' ability to communicate. Even internal communication can be improved with the use of e-mail, allowing administrators and local colleagues to communicate frequently with little cost in time and money.

Numerous studies have found a positive correlation between communication among researchers and their produc-

Changes that decrease the ability of faculty to participate in decision making or the collaborative nature of decision making will negatively affect productivity.

tivity (Aran and Ben-David 1968; Blau 1976; Fox 1991; M. Kelly 1986; Pelz and Andrews 1966). For example, successful scientists frequently describe the benefits of conversations with peers (see, e.g., Sindermann 1985), and the most successful researchers spend significant time (about 15 hours a week) communicating with colleagues (Pelz and Andrews 1966). And a study of the published products of research groups in six countries found that 31 percent of the variance in productivity was explained by communication (both within and between groups) (Visart 1979).

Clearly, it is essential to productivity to provide mechanisms for senior faculty to communicate with each other in person, on the phone, and by e-mail. In times of financial constraints, it is tempting to curtail support for long-distance calls and travel, but such strategies are likely to decrease productivity in both the classroom and the laboratory, especially among those faculty who are most inclined to become isolated (Bergquist, Greenburg, and Klaum 1993) and, as a result, potentially less productive.

Resources

A faculty member's tasks of course require resources in the form of time, space, equipment, supplies, research and project funds, and communication mechanisms. The most crucial resources, however, are people—productive colleagues, quality students, good leaders, and capable staff. Human resources account for the greatest variance in research productivity (Andrews 1979).

As noted earlier, faculty productivity moves up and down depending on the institution where they work, and much of this movement is a function of the colleagues in the institution. While national colleagues are important, local colleagues provide both specific help and a general ambience. Peers play an important role in stimulating vitality by providing a sounding board for new ideas, providing early critiques of writings, serving as guinea pigs for innovative teaching strategies, and providing access to recent findings. To be able to take advantage of this expertise, it helps to have colleagues physically and conceptually close (Blackburn, Behymer, and Hall 1978; Blau 1976). A classic study looked at the correlation between communication and distance between faculty members' office space and found that the probability of communicating with each other was 25 percent if offices were five meters apart but only 8 to 9 percent if they were 10 meters apart (Blackburn, Behymer, and Hall 1978; Blau 1976).

Beyond specific help, productive colleagues can provide meaningful praise, recognition, and support for teaching, research, or committee work. They also maintain the culture and positive climate, perhaps the most important role colleagues play and the way they most positively affect productivity (Reskin 1977). In fact, the absence of research-oriented colleagues destroys the interest in research and the energy of the most productive researchers (Blackburn 1979; Creswell 1985; Meltzer 1956). Being surrounded by faculty who do not value teaching would undoubtedly have the same negative effect on teaching productivity, as Stephen Abbot perhaps discovered.

Quality graduate students (and sometimes undergraduate students) and staff are positively associated with productivity in research. Faculty working with graduate students are much more likely to publish than those working only with undergraduate students (Blackburn, Behymer, and Hall 1978). The presence of able secretarial staff and technicians is highly associated with productivity in research (Pineau and Levy-Leboyer 1983; Sindermann 1985). This finding seems obvious, but today in many institutions, faculty are finding themselves not just without support staff but also having to empty their own wastebaskets and clean their own desks, floors, and windows. These shortages undoubtedly have a negative impact not only on research productivity but also on the enormous efforts faculty are being asked to make to meet the pressing challenges of new technology, diverse student bodies, interdisciplinary research, and course work. For senior faculty, these cutbacks may be particularly disheartening, given their memory of an earlier time when such resources were more readily available.

Size, Age, and Diversity of the Group

Again, most of the research on productivity and organization or group size uses research as the measure of outcome, and much of it is in the natural sciences. This research finds that productivity increases with size of the research group (Blackburn, Behymer, and Hall 1978; Johnston 1994; Jordan, Meador, and Walters 1988; Manis 1951; Pineau and Levy-Leboyer 1983; Smith, Baker, Campbell, and Cunningham 1985; Wispe 1969). In general, with fewer than three to five researchers, students, and staff, research is not very productive. Thereafter, a linear relationship emerges among size of group and accumulated resources, products produced, and recognition received.

An investigation of the impact on research productivity of having members from diverse conceptual and technical backgrounds and their staying together as a group found that, on the whole, being together for a longer length of time is positively associated with the quantity and quality of research (Pelz and Andrews 1966). Nevertheless, when colleagues in the study worked together for over seven years, it was important to attend to maintaining a climate of "creative, supportive tension." Diversity is a positive feature as long as the group has the same primary goals and culture. Senior faculty often play a key role in preserving the group's goals and culture (see also Blau 1976; Pelz 1967; Smith 1971; Steiner 1965).

Rewards

It is clear that senior faculty—like all other faculty—are significantly motivated by intrinsic rewards: being a valued member of the organization, having opportunities to make meaningful contributions, being part of a culture that fits with their values, being part of an organization that has the goal of contributing to society in ways they believe is important, and having autonomy in their jobs (Bowen and Schuster 1986; Eckert and Stecklein 1961; Gustad 1960). Specifically, a study of highly active faculty identified four factors that support successful academic careers: recognition from colleagues and administrators; stimulating colleagues; a strong, academically oriented administration; and adequate resources (Clark and Corcoran 1985).

Fortunately, most senior faculty are satisfied with their autonomy and enthusiastic about their teaching (El-Khawas 1991). They are less satisfied about their working conditions, however (about 63 percent satisfied in one study), teaching load (about 53 percent satisfied), salary and benefits (about 50 percent satisfied), and scholarly opportunities (about 48 percent satisfied). The largest discrepancy in these sources of satisfaction between faculty at two-year and four-year schools is in salary and benefits; 55 percent of faculty in two-year schools in one study were satisfied, compared with only 46 percent of faculty in four-year schools (El-Khawas 1991).

Faculty who most value teaching identify interaction with students as most rewarding. With regard to productivity in research, however, recognition and praise are the most highly rated rewards (Latham and Mitchell 1976). In fact, an experimental study in which researchers were rewarded for productivity with managerial praise, public recognition, or money reveals that all three had a positive impact but that money and praise were most effective. Further, "the increase in performance due to the money over praise was so small as to be practically insignificant. Thus, from a cost/benefit viewpoint, it is most effective to give praise" (Latham and Wexley 1981, p. 190).

Money seems to be an important reward for a small subset of faculty. It is also important when salaries are low (compared with other similar faculty or units) (Blackburn and Pitney 1988; Lewis and Becker 1979). For example, a study of community college faculty found that the primary issue for senior faculty is not salary and that they are adequately paid. Money is important, but it becomes a source of dissatisfaction only when no funds are available for travel, when copy machines do not work, when library holdings become limited, and, in particular, when the lack of funding seems to indicate lack of community or governmental support for the institution or system (Tucker 1990).

Recruitment and Selection

Given that a highly productive organization has clear goals, a distinctive culture that it works to maintain, and a positive climate, it is not surprising that particularly careful and significant time is spent on recruiting and selecting new members of the group (Dill 1985, 1986a, 1986b; Zuckerman 1977). Senior faculty, however, are likely to be well established in the institution and not very likely to move or to be recruited.

Brokered Opportunities for Revitalization

The importance of organizational opportunities for rejuvenating one career's in the continued vitality of faculty has been hypothesized since Rosabeth Moss Kanter detailed the benefits of opportunities for career growth in her now classic *Men and Women of the Corporation* (Kanter 1977; see also Lovett et al. 1984). Conrad Hilberry, a journalist, poet, and professor, describes the importance of opportunities throughout one's career:

Though something similar may be true of other occupa-
tions, I suspect that our job as college teachers is quite
unusual in the amount of room it gives for subcareers
and in the freedom it gives us to choose what subca-
reers we will follow or to shift from one to another. It is
probably unusual, too, in its assumption that our sub-
careers will somehow influence, in a desirable way, the
main business of teaching. To us, as people, these sub-
careers can be wonderfully refreshing and energizing.
From the outside, as my obituary will see it, I was an
English teacher in 1954 and I am an English teacher
today. But from the inside, it's a different life (Lovett et
al. 1984, p. 15).

Recent studies confirm the lack of organizational opportunities and getting "stuck" result in faculty members' becoming disillusioned and less productive (Boice 1986, 1992,
1993). Vital faculty also get stuck but manage to create new
opportunities or are fortunate to have colleagues or department heads who alert them to or encourage them to find
ways to overcome barriers and continue to be productive
(by applying for a fellowship or sabbatical, trying a different
role, team teaching a related course, for example). Being
stuck has a particularly negative impact if it happens early in
a career and the faculty member sees his or her colleagues
continuing on an upward track.

Some are concerned that midcareer faculty will become
stuck if they do not keep up with the continual expansion of
knowledge and technology as their options decrease and as
they proceed through life stages (Finkelstein 1996; Lovett et
al. 1984). To prevent faculty at all levels from becoming stuck,
the institution must take the lead in arranging opportunities
for faculty to continually update their knowledge and skills.

The institution has an essential role in preventing or overcoming stuckness:

Vitality seems to be associated with the availability of
opportunities subject not only to individual motivation
but very much to organizational brokering and entre-
preneurship. . . . The challenge here is one of organiza-
tional development. Senior faculty, especially, need
multifaceted organizational structures that will en-
courage them to broaden their horizons, approach

their work in different and imaginative ways, and find new opportunities to grow and change (Rice and Finkelstein 1993, pp. 14, 17).

Effective Leadership

Given the preceding list of 13 external factors that are important in maintaining faculty members' vitality, it is clear that effective leadership is essential for a vital organization. It is the leaders who can most influence all other institutional variables that facilitate faculty and organizational productivity. "Nearly every positively correlated factor [with productivity] resides in administrative hands" (Blackburn 1979, p. 26). Moreover, in many instances, senior faculty occupy these leadership roles. The next few paragraphs highlight a few key studies that looked specifically at the association of leadership characteristics with research or instructional productivity, and consider how results from these studies pertain directly to senior faculty.

Leaders of productive groups are consistently seen as excellent, productive scientists (Andrews 1979; Biglan 1996; Dill 1982; Sindermann 1985). A study of research groups in Europe found that the leader accounted for much of the variance among groups' productivity (Dill 1982). Further, it was the scientific expertise of the leader that best predicted a group's productivity, suggesting that it is the understanding such a leader brings about the culture, necessary skills, national network, participative decision making, and so on, that allows him or her to best facilitate the group's productivity. Similarly, the climate was most positive in groups where the leader was perceived as highly knowledgeable in the field, technically well qualified, hardworking, and supportive of others' work (Andrews 1979). And a positive group climate correlates positively with productivity (Andrews 1979).

Given what we now know about the features that facilitate productivity, the role of leaders is not surprising. Good leaders are:

. . . highly research oriented (Drew 1985), [internalize] mission and [keep] research emphasis clear to the group (Minckley and Punk 1981), and [exhibit] the behaviors one would expect of a leader with a participative governance style. These behaviors [include] frequent meetings

> **It is the leaders who can most influence all other institutional variables that facilitate faculty and organizational productivity.**

with clear objectives, good leader-member relationships, facilitating open communication [and] allowing expressions of all points of view, complete sharing of information, and vesting ownership of projects with all group members (Birnbaum 1983; Dill 1986[b]; Hoyt and Spangler 1978; Locke, Fitzpatrick, and White 1983; Pelz and Andrews 1966; Pineau and Levy-Leboyer 1983) (Bland and Ruffin 1992, p. 393).

These characteristics are echoed in the literature on effective department heads and higher education leaders (Bensimon, Neumann, and Birnbaum 1989; Lawrence and Blackburn 1985). Studies of the behaviors of effective leaders found two overriding concepts related to effectiveness: initiating structure, and using considerate behaviors (Bensimon, Neumann, and Birnbaum 1989). Initiating structure includes addressing institutional features that facilitate productivity shown in figure 1 (p. 40), particularly establishing clear, coordinating goals, emphasizing top-priority goals, and aligning rewards with goals. Using considerate behaviors includes the same behaviors clustered under "assertive participative governance" (Hemphill 1955; Hoyt and Spangler 1978; Knight and Holen 1985; McCarthy 1972; Skipper 1976).

In short, leaders can greatly influence productivity. And they do so by embodying the values and culture of academe and by attending to the features that facilitate productivity, especially keeping goals visible, initiating structure, using assertive participative leadership, and proactively providing opportunities for advancement and improvement for others. This is a tall order, and the person who might meet these challenges is often over 50, which speaks to the need for senior faculty to remain productive. If they are not, then their colleagues are also less likely to be productive.

These results also suggest the importance of leadership training for senior faculty. While they will likely come to their position of leadership with many desirable characteristics (such as appropriate academic values and experience), they may not be familiar with the features that facilitate productivity or know how to use participative leadership on a grander scale. One study found, for example, that 250 leaders of research and development groups all believed they used participative leadership behaviors but actually exhibited few participative behaviors when meetings conducted by those leaders were taped and the behaviors counted (Argyris 1968).

Conclusions

Knowing that both internal and institutional factors influence faculty members'—and particularly senior faculty members' —productivity and are important for faculty and institutional vitality, one is now in a position to carefully select the individual and institutional strategies most likely to increase vitality.

CONCLUSIONS AND THEMES TO GUIDE APPROACHES TO THE VITALITY OF SENIOR FACULTY

We have arrived at three major conclusions about senior faculty. First, there appears to be no significant decline in competence or productivity as a function of age. Second, the internal and institutional factors outlined in the previous two sections influence faculty productivity at all ages, and they should be addressed to preserve the vitality of senior as well as other faculty. Knowing these factors allows one to monitor them and carefully select the individual and institutional development strategies most likely to simultaneously impact those areas needing attention. Third, while the productivity of senior faculty does not shift downward, a shift does occur in their priorities and values. Understanding these new priorities will be helpful in preserving the vitality of senior faculty.

Beyond these three major conclusions, four themes should be kept in mind in the selection of development strategies:

1. An important interplay occurs between the individual and those institutional factors that facilitate faculty vitality.
2. Faculty vitality is a responsibility of both the individual and the institution.
3. Faculty vitality is best preserved through preventive measures rather than heroic measures to save "stagnant" or "stuck" faculty.
4. Leadership plays a critical role in individual and institutional vitality.

The Interplay between the Individual and the Institution and Their Dual Responsibilities

Prevalent human resource development perspectives in higher education hold that individual and institutional vitality are interrelated and interactive. Broadly speaking, the organization that invests in development and education, that has facilitative organizational policy, and that advances its own employees is operating with a strategy that humans are enhanceable. Such a strategy supports vitality (Clark 1992, p. 1656).

The vitality of individual faculty and the collective vitality of the institution are inseparable. A faculty member cannot long maintain the individual components of vitality (e.g., high morale, commitment, motivation, productive colleagues) without the features of a vital institution (e.g., an appreciative culture, rewards, and opportunities for advancement and improvement). The same is true for the institution: It is not productive or vital without productive, creative faculty. And it is the responsibility of both the faculty member and the university or college to nurture both the individual and the institutional components of faculty development. "Clearly higher education's present and future success . . . depends on the senior faculty. What is all too frequently overlooked, however, is the crucial corollary: *senior faculty members' success . . . depends on the support of their institutions"* (emphasis in the original) (LaCelle-Peterson and Finkelstein 1993, p. 21).

The past has seen little sense of partnership between the institution and the faculty member to accomplish continual individual and institutional vitality. Even though many institutions have offered faculty development programs, faculty have often not seen them as facilitating their continued vitality.

> *There was . . . a prevailing belief that faculty must take care of their own vitality and professional development. As one 15-year humanities instructor explained, "I am highly motivated to seek out and take charge of my own professional development. And it's a good thing I am because no one else is going to do it." Most faculty in the survey did not credit their institutions with much "mentoring" or nurturing when it comes to professional growth* (Tucker 1990, p. 12).

To address faculty and institutional vitality in a meaningful way, faculty and administrators must become informed about the individual and organizational components of vitality and work together to identify which combination of features to focus on for their situation—or multiple situations. While some features that facilitate faculty vitality apply to all faculty, regardless of age, some do not. Younger faculty, for example, need more to acquire initial teaching skills, build their professional network, learn the unwritten rules of their organization, and so on. Senior faculty, on the other hand, may feel stuck, face changing family issues, or feel disillusioned about the gap between their expectations for a career and the reality of their situation.

> *The time is now to give voice to long-standing, age- and career-related issues and concerns and to have them*

taken more seriously by a majority of research universities. To do less is to not understand the overall difficulties and barriers some mid- and late-career faculty are facing to renew their careers and, therefore, possibly transform their lives for the better (Crawley 1995, p. 91).

It is particularly important to pay attention to the institutional features, not because they are more important than the individual features but because they are most often overlooked. A review of the literature on faculty development from the 1960s to the late 1980s found that hundreds of programs and strategies had been used but that "individual-level strategies were discussed eight times more frequently than department-level strategies, and five-and-a-half times more frequently than institution-level strategies" (Bland and Schmitz 1988, pp. 192, 202). Faculty and institutional vitality is a complex, systemic issue that calls for individual, institutional, and integrated approaches.

Preventing Stagnation
"Stagnation" is a word Erikson used to describe a general state of mind and spirit among men and women in the middle of their lives who seem not to be moving ahead in their own development or to be doing much about the development of the next generation or other things about which they care. Specifically, stagnation is manifest in the careers of midlife people when they feel "stuck"—a condition that exists when we feel we are not being very successful in our career and that the prospects of being successful in the near future are not great (Kanter 1977). A somewhat more detailed description of "stuckness" would involve middle-aged and disillusioned faculty who are not only disillusioned with their progress in a career (as Kanter suggests), but also have a low sense of self-worth, are disengaged from their department and profession, are unproductive as scholars, researchers, and creators, and have become isolated from colleagues and students (Boice 1993).

"Stuckness," Kanter suggests, is a relative term: We compare ourselves to other people with whom we work and feel that time is passing us by, that we have no career opportunities, that we are always bumping our heads against either a highly visible ceiling or (especially in the case of many women and minorities) an invisible "glass" ceiling.

Being stuck does not necessarily mean that we feel insecure in our jobs. In fact, we often feel stuck precisely because we do not feel free to leave our secure, often highly paid, jobs to find work that we enjoy and that will give us a greater sense of achievement. When senior faculty become stuck and disillusioned, they do not leave and they are not fired. Instead, they become burdens to their institutions. They are unsociable and oppositional and do not shoulder their fair share of departmental duties (Boice 1993).

Only a "small minority" of senior faculty at the major research university in one study exhibited characteristics of being "stuck." These faculty had:

> . . . become disenchanted with academe. Although they have had relative success in the system, they seem to have lost their professional zeal. Their work is less meaningful, and they are not responsive to the demands of the institution. They often express cynicism and boredom. In part, their disenchantment is a result of some earlier failures or disappointments. Those who personally chose to emphasize teaching express a resentment toward the university, which "puts too much emphasis on research" (Braskamp et al. 1982, p. 22).

These faculty are not, however, dissatisfied; they derive most of their satisfaction from their personal life—family, friends, traveling, or sports (Braskamp et al. 1982).

From the specific and narrow perspective of their institution, these faculty members are "stagnant." They have met all of Erikson's criteria for stagnation: They no longer find any fulfillment in their work, blame others for their own failures, look with resentment or disdain at the accomplishments of their colleagues (especially those younger than themselves), and fall into a stance of cynicism and boredom. How does an institution try to revive the vitality of these stuck or stagnant faculty members? Although the institution would label these faculty "stuck," they are not stagnant in their lives—only in their careers. Vitalization for these faculty might therefore not be the central issue. It might instead be how to bring the shifting interests of some senior faculty into the institution. Or, more precisely, how do we expand our own sense of the mission and boundaries of our institution so that it embraces a new set of roles and opportunities for senior faculty? If a senior faculty member enjoys a renewed interest in sports, then how do we integrate this interest into the current activities of our college? If a professor wants to spend more time with his family, then how do we enable the family to become more fully a part of our university?

Clearly, recapturing the interest of stuck faculty is very difficult. Thus, the institution would be wise to strive to *prevent* stuckness or stagnation, and guidance on how to do so comes from two studies (Boice 1993; Corcoran and Clark 1985). Corcoran and Clark's study involved a group of highly active and vital faculty members and a group of "representative faculty" at the University of Minnesota. The highly active and vital faculty members had not gone through their careers untouched by barriers and disappointments. "The experience of career blockage is one that most faculty members will experience at some point in their careers. How they view the experience, to what they attribute it, and how they address it now [seem] to be what is significant for understanding faculty vitality" (Corcoran and Clark 1985, p. 69).

Virtually all the faculty interviewed at the University of Minnesota identified one or more career blocks. They had plateaued as researchers, had had to set aside research projects to take on administrative work, had ceased to be attractive to funding agencies, had failed to receive support from colleagues for their research, had been unsuccessful in completing a major research project, or had been unable to successfully shift to a new project. The highly active faculty members, however, were eventually able to make the necessary shifts in their priorities and activities. It is particularly noteworthy that these generative faculty members:

> . . . *tended to take a more active problem-solving approach [than did their more stagnant colleagues], rooted in a realistic understanding of the circumstances of academic life. Some also showed a maturing concern for helping younger colleagues and graduate students in shaping their careers, expressing a concern for "generative" responsibilities and for serving appropriately in mentor relationships* (Corcoran and Clark 1985, p. 72).

Thus, faculty can avoid becoming stuck by being armed with strategies, or assisted by administrators in identifying strategies, to overcome their career blocks, such as reaching out to other people as teachers, sponsors, and mentors, and by embracing a wide range of interests, thereby being able to move elsewhere when stuck in any one project.

Similarly, guidance on how to prevent stuckness can be derived from Boice's study (1993), in which he interviewed a stagnant group of faculty who had been identified as middle-aged and disillusioned (MADFs) and a generative group who were considered exemplary and productive. The MADFs were found to have a low sense of self-worth and to be disengaged from their department and profession, unproductive as scholars, and isolated from colleagues and students. Further, MADFs had experienced crucial events during the first years of their academic careers that they interpreted as collegial isolation or neglect and collegial disapproval. These experiences, in turn, left them with self-doubts about competence, feelings of victimization, and a suspicious attitude. In contrast, senior faculty identified as exemplary performers by their department chairs found strong social networks when they arrived on campus and acceptance from their students. These faculty were immediately successful in writing grant proposals, publishing the results of their research, and finding opportunities to consult or travel early in their careers. These findings suggest that crucial events early in one's career are a major cause of later disillusionment (in the case of MADFs) or success (in the case of exemplary performers).

The key questions then become how to help young faculty deal constructively with crucial events affecting their careers and thus avoid getting stuck. Or, once stuck and disillusioned, how do faculty get reengaged? Boice found an answer to the second question—at least for the MADFs with whom he was working—asking them to participate as mentors in a project where senior faculty were paired with junior faculty. This acknowledgment of their value to others resulted in significant positive changes in their behavior in their departments and toward their department chairs and colleagues. Nevertheless, while devising strategies for salvaging stuck faculty members is important, proactively preventing stuckness would be much more productive. Strategies for prevention include helping junior faculty avoid negative events, if possible, but, when they do happen, coaching them on how to handle them as opportunities for growth.

Leadership

Leaders in higher education have increasingly complex roles. Not only must they interact with and support their faculty; they are also asked to work with many types of staff, manage sophisticated budgets, work with external constituencies, and more. Now, we are also asking them to understand the individual and organizational features that facilitate productivity, which includes some understanding of adult and career development. And we are asking them to actively assist individual faculty in maintaining vitality and alter institutional features to maintain collective faculty vitality. Certainly, such leaders need formal training and perhaps incentives to maintain senior faculty members' vitality, rather than "shedding" the faculty members.

Summary

Because of the interplay between institutional and individual features of vitality, vitality is optimally facilitated by an integrated approach that simultaneously addresses both types of features, attending particularly to the varied needs of faculty at different stages of their careers and development.

The best faculty development program is proactive and preventive.

Thus, the best faculty development program is proactive and preventive. The health-care industry is finding that good health is facilitated, and costs are contained, by promoting healthy lifestyles and by screening for potential problems to prevent disease or addressing problems early when they are most treatable. Similarly, continually monitoring and attending to the needs of individual faculty and higher education institutions can do much to ensure their health and to ensure that fewer resources need be spent on "rescuing" faculty. How does one continually monitor the vitality of each faculty member and institutional factor and attend to the vitality of both before they become problems? We turn to the answers in the final section of this monograph.

It is quite clear that the environment of the institution where senior faculty work affects the quality of their work, the attention and service they provide to the institution, and their own sense of self as an academic professional—just as it does any other faculty member. "Environmental factors can affect faculty morale, commitment to the institution, and, consequently, productivity" (Gill et al. 1992, p. 5). The key environmental factors for senior faculty appear to be opportunities for growth (Baldwin and Blackburn 1981), a sense of being appreciated by the leaders of the institution and a sense of collegiality (Bowen and Schuster 1986), and a sense of commitment by the leaders of the institution to the college's or university's founding mission (Tucker 1990). The portrait of Stephen Abbot is of a man who is struggling to remain vital in an institution that he perceives no longer appreciates his contributions, lacks a sense of collegiality, and has abandoned a commitment to innovation in general and educational innovation in particular. If circumstances remain unchanged, through Abbot's inaction as well as his organization's apparent lack of interest, Abbot could readily become disenchanted. The marginalization of Stephen Abbot —and other senior faculty like him—would be a profound loss to his university as it prepares for the next millennium.

The sense of appreciation for Stephen Abbot and other senior faculty need not be expressed through salary increases (Bowen and Schuster 1986). Senior faculty recognize that they are usually at the top of the pay scale and that their merits can no longer be acknowledged with money. Moreover, in many instances, senior faculty are not as financially hard-pressed as they once were when they were building their families and social networks along with their careers. Appreciation for senior faculty like Abbot often can come through other means. Opportunities for professional development are signs of appreciation, as are institutional programs that feature such initiatives as partially reimbursed sabbaticals, flexible teaching schedules, late-career grant programs, retraining, and early retirement (although early retirement programs can be demeaning if they are inadequately designed and promoted).

Traditional Approaches to Faculty Vitality

When faculty in liberal arts colleges were asked to identify critical events that have significantly influenced their careers, they:

*. . . frequently described opportunities for professional
growth (e.g., sabbaticals, workshops, research projects,
independent study grants). In the latter four career
stages, the proportion of faculty mentioning growth
opportunities ranged from 59 percent of experienced
assistant professors . . . to 91 percent of continuing full
professors* (Baldwin and Blackburn 1981, p. 607).

One can conclude from these findings that faculty in liberal
arts colleges see the beneficial effects of opportunities to
expand their professional capabilities. Moreover, these faculty may begin to fully appreciate these benefits only at the
latter stages of their careers. It is ironic that senior faculty
may be beneficiaries of the least amount of professional
development services precisely at the point in their careers
when they appreciate them most.

Do these findings hold up with faculty in other kinds of
institutions? And how active are senior faculty with regard to
professional development? They may recognize the value of
these programs, but do they have the time (or sufficient interest) to participate in them? Although some evidence suggests that senior faculty are less likely to participate in formal professional development activities than their younger
colleagues (Baldwin 1990, p. 30), other evidence is somewhat contradictory (El-Khawas 1991). Based on 1989 results
from the Higher Education Research Institute, a large proportion of senior faculty participated in faculty development
programs at their institutions during the previous two years,
the proportion being much higher (75 percent) for senior
faculty at two-year institutions than for those at four-year
colleges and universities (46 percent) (El-Khawas 1991, p.
7). In the case of both two-year and four-year institutions,
the level of participation for senior faculty was close to the
level for all faculty.

Most senior faculty members also "regularly attend professional meetings away from campus, but typically for only a
few days each year" (El-Khawas 1991, p. 7). Once again, the
level of participation by senior faculty at two-year and four-
year institutions varies considerably, with senior faculty at
four-year institutions devoting more time than those at two-
year institutions to professional activities away from campus.
Among senior faculty at four-year institutions, 30 percent
indicate that they devote five to 10 days each year to profes-

sional activities, whereas only 21 percent of senior faculty at two-year institutions spend five to 10 days away on professional activities. At the lower end of the spectrum, 36 percent of senior faculty at four-year institutions devote one to four days to professional activities, while 51 percent of senior faculty at two-year institutions devote one to four days each year to professional activities. Only 13 percent of the senior faculty at four-year institutions indicate that they spend no time on professional activities. In contrast, 21 percent of the senior faculty at two-year institutions report no days away for these activities.

Based on a study of developmental shifts over time among liberal arts faculty, no one professional development program will appeal to all faculty members (Baldwin and Blackburn 1981). In his early years, Stephen Abbot was enthralled with instructional innovation. Axelrod used him as an example of the professor who cared about his students and explored new teaching methods and style. Yet now, in the 1990s, Abbot would probably be one of the last faculty members at his university to volunteer for a new program on instructional innovation. If invited to lead such a program, however, Abbot might once again become interested, for vital involvement often begins with the act of appreciation (Srivastva, Cooperider, and Associates 1990). He would probably not, however, view such a program as responsive to his own current interests.

Each faculty member must be treated as a distinctive individual whose needs and interests will shift over time. Senior faculty like Abbot often prefer opportunities for growth that "they can design and carry out at their own pace," whereas younger faculty may prefer formal workshops and seminars that provide colleagueship and support as well as knowledge and skills (Baldwin and Blackburn 1981, p. 611). Institutions that offer nothing more than instructional improvement programs do not address the primary needs of many faculty—especially senior faculty like Abbot: "Except in the first year or two, teaching is a smaller concern than, say, an unfilled desire to make a contribution to one's field. Higher education institutions now need to broaden their focus to include the professional, organizational, and personal development of faculty" (p. 608). While this study can be faulted for leaping to such a broad conclusion based on only a study of faculty from one specific kind of institution (prestigious liberal arts colleges), many other professional development practitioners have argued for years that an effective faculty development program should address many different dimensions of a faculty member's life (see, e.g., Bergquist 1981).

The results of this study also suggest that faculty may need considerable support from administrators and colleagues at certain points in their careers and very little assistance at other points. "Faculty performance might be improved by easing some responsibilities (e.g., committee assignments) or providing some additional support (e.g., secretarial help, research assistance)" during the particularly stressful periods of transition (Baldwin and Blackburn 1981, p. 611). Conversely, during more tranquil periods, faculty might be given particularly challenging assignments: "A new administrative task or community service project may inject a sufficient dose of variety to enliven the routine of an established college teacher" (p. 611). Given that students' learning and development tend to occur at those points in their lives when there is a balance between challenge and support (Sanford 1980), perhaps we should offer senior faculty support during times when their careers are being most fully challenged and challenges when their careers are relatively quiet and filled with supportive structures (Baldwin and Blackburn 1981). Faculty should also be given the opportunity to participate in career-planning activities that they can adapt:

> . . . consciously and systematically to personal and institutional changes. . . . Understanding the career as an evolutionary process permits a professor to anticipate and prepare for vocational changes. Planned career development should be more rational and rewarding than evolution stimulated by chance opportunities and routine periods of dissatisfaction. . . . Professors should regularly assess what they have achieved professionally, where they are headed, and how these factors match with their personal values and goals (Baldwin and Blackburn 1981, pp. 611–12).

These career-planning activities should be supplemented and supported by flexible leave policies and opportunities for internships.

A Comprehensive Approach to Faculty Vitality*

Preserving the vitality of senior faculty clearly requires attending to the multiple factors that affect vitality. Thus, to maintain faculty and institutional vitality, specific people at the institution, college, and department should be assigned to monitor the individual and institutional factors that facilitate vitality and to address the ones found to be weak. At the institutional level, this person would likely be the vice president for human resources or the vice president for faculty affairs, that is, the person responsible for facilitating faculty and organizational vitality.

While traditional faculty development often acknowledged and was built on many individual features of vitality, it usually lacked an institutional or systems approach. Believing one's efforts contribute to a larger goal is a powerful personal motivator (Locke and Latham 1984). On the other hand, from the organization's point of view, why support individual renewal if it does not contribute to the accomplishment of the organization's larger mission? This essential link between an individual's goals and his or her development and the institution's goals (see, e.g., Bland and Schmitz 1986; Votruba 1990) brings us back to the institutional portion of the model in figure 1 (p. 40). As previously described, research finds that it is necessary but not sufficient for a faculty member to possess the individual characteristics listed in the model; to be highly productive, the faculty member must also be a member of an organization that has the features and leadership listed in the model. In sum, to maintain the productivity of older faculty members—as well as their younger colleagues' future productivity—a comprehensive approach is required that addresses: (1) the individual's goals, motivation, life stage, competencies, and interests; (2) the organization's goals, leadership strategies, culture, policies, and resources, and the systems that affect productivity; and (3) the essential link between these factors.

Nearly all writers discussing vitality stress that various strategies are needed to address the varied needs of these faculty members who come from various disciplines, are at different stages in their careers, and bring distinctive personal circumstance (see, e.g., Bergquist 1981; Bergquist and Phillips

To maintain the productivity of older faculty members— as well as their younger colleagues' future productivity —a comprehensive approach is required.

*Portions of this subsection were drawn, with permission, from C.J. Bland, June 1997, "Beyond Corporate Downsizing: A Better Way for Medical Schools to Succeed in a Changing World," *Academic Medicine* 72(6): 13–19.

1977; Bland and Ridky 1993; Wheeler and Schuster 1990). Bergquist and Phillips (1975a, 1975b) advocated a comprehensive approach more than 20 years ago, suggesting that effective instructional and, more broadly, professional development will be successful and sustained over many years only if coupled with effective personal and organizational development programs. Since the 1970s, however, most colleges and universities have focused primarily on instructional improvement, with some professional development (usually within the discipline) thrown in for good measure (Bland and Schmitz 1988). Very little has been done in the area of personal development, other than some efforts at interdisciplinary dialogue and an occasional life or career planning workshop.

The similar failure of most colleges and universities to embrace the organizational development components of a comprehensive faculty development program is evident in the finding in 1985 that recommendations for faculty development up to that point "typically [focused] on efforts to change the individual in some manner, but ignored the organizational and institutional contexts that shape and structure faculty careers" (Corcoran and Clark 1985, p. 58).

In addition to not being comprehensive, attempts at faculty development are usually not coordinated. Universities, schools, or departments frequently offer a hodgepodge of structural changes and development strategies that have a much smaller impact than would a similar number of efforts guided by an overall plan. Instead, as an alternative to this hodgepodge, we offer a comprehensive approach to human and organizational development that provides a rational foundation for selecting a combination of individual and organizational activities that together will have a larger impact (Bergquist, Phillips, and Gruber 1992; Bland and Ridky 1993).

This comprehensive approach begins with the understanding that the purpose of a human and organizational development program for collegiate institutions is quite simple—to facilitate faculty members' and the staff's commitment and ability to achieve their own career goals and their institution's goals by (1) continually assisting and developing all employees (new and experienced, administrative and nonadministrative) in areas related to both their goals and the institution's goals and (2) continually improving the organizational features that facilitate quality work. These features include, for example, clear organizational goals, structures and mechanisms that coordinate individual goals and organizational goals, equitable personnel policies, effective reward structures, and a supportive climate.

A university or college should ultimately aim for a comprehensive human resource program that addresses all employees at all career stages and that continually assesses and modifies its organizational structure and processes. Realistically, most organizations must choose from a comprehensive approach where to put the majority of their development efforts at any given time. But having in mind a comprehensive approach allows one to select the best place to focus efforts and when and where the focus of these efforts should change.

What is a comprehensive plan? A comprehensive plan for human and organizational development addresses the three key aspects of an organization: the attitudes of people who perform the work (goals, values, morale, culture, expectations, dreams), the processes used to perform the work (teaching, research, writing, advising), and the structures designed to facilitate the work (reward structures, lines of authority, procedures, functional units). Anything that has an impact on any one of these aspects eventually affects the other two. How does such a comprehensive plan work? To address these three key aspects of an organization, three broad development approaches have been used over the years: organizational development, personal development, and functional development.

The organizational development approach assumes that people and organizations are improved by focusing on issues larger than the individual person; hence, shifts in organizationwide structures, processes, and attitudes (culture) are emphasized rather than individual factors. In contrast, the personal development approach assumes that personal characteristics are all-important. People bring to the organization not just their job skills, but also certain characteristics and circumstances that affect their professional productivity, such as interpersonal skills, financial status, habits and prejudices, family situations, and plans for their lives and careers. From the perspective of personal development, we influence and improve organizational functioning by improving the personal conditions and perspectives of those who work in the organization. The functional development approach brings together the individual and the organization. This approach concentrates on equipping people with the skills, attitudes, and knowledge required to be continually productive in a changing organization. It emphasizes both the assessment of job performance and its improvement.

These three approaches to human and organizational development are graphically represented in figure 4. The columns show general examples of the strategies the three dominant approaches use to address an organization's three key aspects. "Diagnosis/assessment" provides examples of the types of methods each development approach uses to assess the current level of development of the individual or organization. Ideally, an organization constantly conducts assessments to guide where it needs to put development efforts. Figure 5 offers an even more detailed list of activities that colleges and universities can use with regard to each of the three approaches.

FIGURE 4

A Comprehensive Model for the Development Of Human and Organizational Resources

Organizational Features	Development Approaches		
	Organizational Development	*Personal Development*	*Functional Development*
Attitude	Organizational culture interventions	Creativity/sensitivity development workshops Personal counseling	Employee motivation programs Employee transitions programs
Process	Vision building Team building	Interpersonal skills training Self-management workshops	Technical training Management skills development
Structure	Reengineering Restructuring Personnel policies/ procedures redesign	Employee support services	Job planning and design Incentive planning and design
Diagnosis/ Assessment	Organizational diagnosis	Life/career planning	Performance appraisal

Note: See figure 5 for a more detailed list of strategies for each development approach.
Sources: Adapted from Bergquist, Phillips, and Gruber 1992, and from Bland 1997.

Typically, development efforts are initiated in an uncoordinated fashion as a result of a crisis, individual agendas, or funding requirements or opportunities. For example, most medical schools recently established courses on the responsible conduct of research because of NIH's requirement or because of notoriety from recent cases involving fraud in research. Similarly, colleges have offered courses on teaching or curriculum design as a result of a foundation's call for such proposals. They are all worthy and important efforts toward development, but they most likely were not initiated as a result of carefully deciding which efforts would best facilitate faculty and institutional vitality or best enable individuals to accomplish their goals or collectively realize the university's vision. Taking an integrated approach that identifies the areas that simultaneously need to be addressed to facilitate individual and collective productivity will increase many times over the impact of singular, uncoordinated efforts. (Examples of strategies for monitoring institutional features and identifying the areas that need attention are listed in figure 5.)

Monitoring the individual features that facilitate productivity is more difficult. How can an institution attend to the many individual features that vary across, for example, age, discipline, career stage, and gender and still be manageable? One way is to focus on helping faculty examine their own circumstances and needs. Thus, the organization does not offer all types of "faculty development" programs but rather assists faculty in forming their yearly goals and what is needed to meet those goals, and then serves as a locator or clearinghouse to other resources to meet the identified needs. This strategy works best when the institution and its departments have organizational goals within which individual faculty members or faculty teams write yearly work plans and when they reward accomplishment of yearly plans through public recognition, advancement, and salary increases (Wergin 1994).

Such a strategy provides the link between the individual and the organization. It provides a mechanism for the individual to feel a part of and contribute to the organization while simultaneously building the rationale for why the organization should commit resources to the individual's goals. Further, yearly plans ensure that faculty emerge productive in their senior years, thereby preventing stuckness and maintaining momentum and competitiveness. Finally, this strategy

FIGURE 5

A Sample of Activities for Each Developmental Approach

Organizational Development

- Clarify institutional (and collegiate and departmental) mission and vision.
- Assure (not simply allow) participation in governance.
- Develop and encourage institutional leadership by faculty.
- Proactively arrange opportunities for development for faculty, e.g., fellowships, sabbaticals, loans to corporations, faculty exchanges.
- Provide opportunities for faculty to serve as mentors.
- Moderate cultural conflicts in institution.
- Develop and maintain common academic values.
- Revise personnel policies and procedures, addressing the problems of variable benefits and appointments.
- Review the adequacy and equity of salaries.
- Initiate opportunities for post-tenure review and link them to faculty development.

Personal Development

- Offer training in interpersonal skills.
- Offer financial planning workshops and consultation.
- Offer cross-cultural training.
- Provide required courses on recognizing and avoiding sexual harassment.
- Help faculty identify need for and sources of personal counseling.
- Create in-house child-care services.
- Offer career counseling.
- Offer life- and career-planning workshops.
- Provide a career-alternatives program that encourages the exploration of nontraditional functions.
- Offer fitness and wellness programs.
- Provide opportunities for part-time employment.
- Provide options for early retirement.

works best when the organizational representative (e.g., department head or faculty developer) who works with faculty in establishing goals is aware of life stages and helps the individual also recognize and capitalize on these characteristics in their plans.

Ideally, faculty would be asked to write goals in a somewhat measurable form for each year. These goals should be related to the college's broader goals and to the mission of the department and the division in which the faculty members teach, as well as to the individual's goals and circum-

Functional Development

- Provide technical training for faculty.
- Provide training in curriculum design.
- Offer in-service courses on the responsible conduct of research.
- Offer leadership development programs.
- Offer workshops on presentation skills.
- Offer workshops on instructional skills.
- Provide workshops and consultation on instructional technology.
- Support attendance at national disciplinary meetings.
- Initiate instructional evaluation systems.
- Fund advanced-degree programs for faculty.

Diagnosis/Assessment

Organizational Development

- Conduct morale and climate surveys.
- Conduct institutional comparison studies.
- Conduct exit interviews.
- Track number of academic misconduct and senate judicial cases.
- Use employees' evaluations of systems, e.g., financial, human resources, salary.

Personal Development

- Analyze faculty self-reports for annual goal statements and year-end meetings.
- Track number of sexual harassment cases.
- Track reasons for missed work.

Functional Development

- Use faculty self-reports in annual goal statements and year-end meetings.
- Conduct post-tenure reviews.
- Conduct student or peer assessments of teaching.
- Track number of grants/patents acquired.
- Conduct annual assessment of administrators.

stances. And each year at least one goal should be aimed at updating one's abilities. Obsolescence is inevitable unless the individual, with the help of the organization, continuously and systematically works at staying up to date in his or her content and technical areas. Before submitting these goals to the department chair or head, each person should formally discuss his or her goals with at least two other departmental faculty members.

This discussion is recommended as a result of studies on productive research organizations (Andrews 1979), which found that the most productive ones had a system in which more than one person contributed to a scientist's work plan (although the scientist had the final say). This step also facilitates the use of colleagues' knowledge of one's abilities, future needs, and available resources in setting goals. It also ensures that colleagues will know about what others are doing; thus, they can serve as immediate reminders of goals established and as informed celebrants of accomplishments. Further, it places subtle peer pressure on staying up to date and productive. Finally, this approach relieves the department chair or head of being the only "heavy" to expect reasonable goals and accomplishments or be the only source of recognition for accomplishing goals. On the other hand, it provides the faculty member support for his or her plan in negotiations with the department chair or head.

For the same reasons, faculty members' end-of-year reports on goals accomplished should be periodically reviewed by faculty peers in addition to the department chair or head (Edwards 1994).

In return for developing yearly career plans that meet both individual and organizational needs, the faculty member receives a commitment from the organization for essential resources or training needed to accomplish the plan and, when appropriate, help in identifying and obtaining resources or training. In return for accomplishing yearly plans, the faculty member should receive satisfaction, recognition, and other valued rewards. These plans and the year-end review of how well goals have been met, and an agreed-upon reward structure provide the framework for an automatic but individualized system of faculty development, motivation, and evaluation.

Features of Individual, Institutional, and Leadership Vitality Likely to Need Attention

By continually monitoring individual's and leaders' vitality and by requiring each faculty member to include a development goal in his or her yearly plan, the institution is alerted to areas it should address proactively to facilitate faculty and institutional success. In the past, colleges and universities have found that a significant number of faculty members want to enhance their abilities in a few consistent areas each year—perhaps computer skills, curriculum design, teaching strategies such as problem-based learning, collaborative learning, and computer-assisted instruction, or writing.

Many institutions are redefining their missions and goals, losing the cohesion of their culture, struggling with decreasing resources (people, equipment, and dollars), facing declining physical facilities and decreased morale among faculty, and so on. Thus, there is likely also to be a common subset of institutional features that need attention. Specifically, with regard to the sustained vitality of senior faculty, we suspect many institutions will find they particularly need to attend to institutional purpose, positive institutional climate, morale, maintenance of basic academic values, participative governance, the abilities of leaders, and the maintenance of competence.

By way of illustration, the following paragraphs briefly discuss the conditions common to many institutions regarding senior faculty members' morale and institutional climate.

Faculty morale

Among the idealistic young faculty of the 1960s—men and women like Stephen Abbot—it was widely assumed that abundant financial support would be present indefinitely and that American colleges and universities would continue to embrace innovation and continuous improvement. Only in the late 1970s and early 1980s were these assumptions fully challenged. Impatient young faculty during the 1970s would complain about minor drops in funding for their divisions or about a reduction in the rate of budgetary growth in their institutions. They would grow frustrated with the seemingly slow rate of innovation in their departments.

These minor disappointments and frustrations, however, would soon seem trivial when compared to the much more significant ramifications that confronted faculty members in the 1980s and 1990s. As usual, we do not know that we have lived through the "good old days" until we are faced with the new realities of our present time. Like Stephen Abbot, many faculty members faced disillusionment and a sense of personal disengagement during the 1980s at a time in their lives when they would expect to be most influential in their colleges and universities. Ironically, as Abbot discovered, they may have actually been more influential earlier in their careers.

Now, some senior faculty feel unappreciated by administrators of their institutions and have ceased to believe that their institutions are places that can be improved and again made vital. Abbot seems to be discouraged. He finds some satisfaction in his teaching to particularly bright students but holds little hope for renewed public support for his institution or renewed wisdom on the part of his university's faculty and administrative leaders. While faculty like Abbot may not themselves be burned out and may in fact play effective, generative roles in their institutions, it is often in spite of, not because of, the institution. Thus, we fail to honor the founders of our institutions (in the case of community colleges) or those who have led us through the difficult years of growth and retrenchment (in the case of four-year institutions). When we fail to recognize these contributions from the past, we also minimize the chances of significant contributions in the near future from senior colleagues.

It is of course hard for anyone to maintain high morale and to live and work productively and collaboratively in an organization that fails to appreciate his or her efforts. It is particularly hard, however, for the senior members of colleges and universities. Moreover, mature men and women like Abbot are less inclined to tolerate these slights. We are more inclined in our senior years to reject inconsiderate behavior and hassles, and so we tend to avoid committees, interpersonal conflicts, and campus politics (Bergquist, Greenburg, and Klaum 1993). Midcareer faculty in the social sciences and humanities find it increasingly difficult to tolerate "endless committees and paperwork" (Tucker 1990, p. 8). And "senior professors appear more likely to solve problems independently than do their junior colleagues" (Baldwin 1990, p. 30).

Institutional climate

Perhaps most important to senior faculty is the environment we create that encourages their own ongoing development and, in turn, their own internally motivated desire for productivity. Stephen Abbot may not need a professional development program. What he may need instead is an appreciative and supportive environment for his own individual pursuit of new ideas (such as postmodernism) or new modes of teaching. Said one community college faculty member, "I can take care of my own renewal, but I need to surround myself with kindred spirits, and I need administrators and people that understand what I do and trust that I am doing my job. Camaraderie is the single most important word that sums up what I need" (Tucker 1990, pp. 16–17). Thus, it is important to attend to the culture and climate in the organization as well as to the perceived mechanism for individual support.

Strategies for Addressing the Vitality of Individuals, Institutions, and Leaders

This discussion of senior faculty with regard to morale and the institutional climate illustrates that the features of the individual, the institution, and its leaders that predict and facilitate faculty productivity are not independent. Listing them separately in figure 1 allows us to display the features for discussion and more accurately reflects how they are studied. But they are quite interdependent. The disadvantage of this interdependence is that if one or two features become weak or negative, it simultaneously negatively affects many other features and ultimately faculty productivity. This domino effect was seen most recently on campuses where governing boards tried to weaken tenure codes, decrease security in a position, and streamline procedures for removing faculty. Faculty understand this approach as disregard for the culture and values of the academic profession, especially academic freedom, peer review, and participative governance. This perceived decline in the appreciation of the academic culture results in the simultaneous effect of significantly lowered faculty morale, institutional climate, participative governance, and so on. Thus, it appears that a productive institution relies on the presence of multiple features that singularly are quite fragile. But when most of them are strong and positive, they provide the foundation for a highly productive, robust institution.

The advantage of the features' high degree of interconnectedness is that the strategies that improve one feature positively affect others. Having an *institutional* office to address weak features that affect vitality can be an effective way to implement strategies that simultaneously and positively affect multiple features. Such an office also provides evidence of the institution's commitment to and support of the continuous improvement required to avoid obsolescence and remain productive. It is also efficient for addressing common faculty or leadership development needs and institutional development. In fact, a review of strategies affecting

A productive institution relies on multiple features that singularly are quite fragile. But when most of them are strong and positive, they provide the foundation for a highly productive institution.

faculty and institutional vitality found that institutional strategies to promote productivity are becoming more frequently used than are individual or departmental approaches (Bland and Schmitz 1990). For example, the most recently used strategy was "alternative personnel policies," such as "midcareer change (either to another career or to new duties), early retirement and buyout options . . . , flexible benefits . . . , early recruitment of faculty from graduate school . . . , flexible staffing patterns . . . , time-shared positions . . . , and combinations" of them (pp. 52, 56).

Institutional offices could, however, appear disconnected from, or irrelevant to, some faculty members. To avoid this perception, strategies such as liaisons to each department or college or an advisory committee of influential faculty members are recommended. Or the institutional office could serve as a coordinating umbrella over multiple local programs to take advantage of existing programs and use their collective strength to address faculty or institutional needs (Watson and Grossman 1994).

Despite the fact that the needs of individuals, institutions, and leaders of each organization will be somewhat peculiar to that organization, there will also likely be common needs across institutions. Some general development strategies will be useful in addressing these common needs; they are described in the next subsections, specifically institutional policies on and opportunities for or approaches to institutional leadership by faculty, mentoring colleagues, early retirement, career alternatives, linking faculty evaluation and development, proactive arrangement of opportunities for development, faculty renewal in content and technical skills, and development for administrators.*

Institutional leadership by senior faculty
Institutional vitality in the next century clearly remains in the hands of those men and women who at a much younger

_____
*These subsections provide general descriptions of the strategies. For descriptions of actual faculty and institutional development programs, readers should turn to such sources as Boice 1992, Finkelstein and LaCelle-Peterson 1993, Schuster and Wheeler 1990, Seagren, Creswell, and Wheeler 1993, and the annual *To Improve the Academy: Resources for Faculty, Instructional, and Organizational Development* published by the Professional and Organizational Development Network in Higher Education. An ERIC search on areas needing attention will quickly identify dozens of highly relevant articles, including the most recent innovations in faculty development. Other databases, particularly Medline and Psych Abstracts, will also provide information.

age forged the distinctive character of contemporary American higher education. Those men and women who joined four-year colleges and universities during the late 1960s and early 1970s as young and idealistic faculty members overwhelmed the established professoriat in both numbers and enthusiasm. They had not only new ideas, but also access to much more substantial financial resources, student enrollments, and public support than ever before in American higher education.

For those faculty members who entered two-year community colleges in the late 1960s and early 1970s, an even greater opportunity often presented itself to immediately provide institutional leadership, for in many instances they were among the founders of the college or at least were warmly welcomed by other relatively young faculty who were founding members. Those young idealists looked forward to gaining assistance from other youthful colleagues who shared similar populist dreams of providing high-quality education to those who had previously been under-served in their communities. Today, senior faculty once again have been given the opportunity to exert significant leadership in their institutions. They must once again play a critical role in transforming American higher education for the next generation of students and the next millennium:

The senior faculty now in place constitutes the largest faculty cohort in the history of American higher education. This group of professors provided leadership in shaping the basic character of American colleges and universities in the second half of the twentieth century and will also play a pivotal role in selecting the faculty who will lead us into the new century. If American higher education is to be fundamentally altered over the next several years, the present cohort of senior faculty will be immensely influential in shaping the future (Rice and Finkelstein 1993, p. 7).

Whether for good or ill, the faculty who are now in or entering their senior years profoundly changed American colleges and universities during the late 1960s and early 1970s. Strategies should be implemented to ensure they play a critical leadership role again and serve as mentors to those who are younger or less experienced in the complexities of institutional governance, curriculum planning, and campus politics.

Mentoring colleagues

The senior years are apparently a perfect time to encourage the mentoring of younger colleagues, given the orientation of many faculty during these years toward generativity. While senior faculty may be a little tired of directing their generativity toward the teaching of undergraduate or graduate students, as they typically have been doing for many years, the prospect of helping a young faculty member (or an older faculty member who has just entered the academy after a career outside higher education) is likely to be new and exciting.

Not only are many senior faculty oriented toward the mentoring of colleagues, but they also are invaluable to the process because no one else in the institution knows it quite like they do. Given the large turnover in faculty expected with the retirement of many senior faculty and the necessary recruitment of many new faculty into institutions that may actually be growing again, the role of mentor is crucial: "Preparation for this eventual turnover in the faculty ranks must include consideration of how today's senior faculty can provide the models, the supporting policies, and the appropriate reward structures to socialize tomorrow's new faculty into the teaching role"—as well as other roles in the institution (Finkelstein and LaCelle-Peterson 1993, p. 1). A faculty member like Stephen Abbot has learned much over his many years of service that can be conveyed to younger faculty. We have learned from Axelrod's portrayal of Abbot over 30 years; couldn't his younger colleagues also learn from him?

Mentoring can take many different forms. It can literally mean teaching other faculty how to perform a specific function, or it can mean coaching or counseling less experienced faculty in their work at the institution as teachers, committee members, researchers, scholars, and so on. Mentoring can also involve serving as role models. Typically, senior faculty themselves never received much orientation when they first entered the academy, usually as newly minted Ph.D.s or professionals with little academic experience.

Today's senior faculty were hired in a period when socialization to the teaching role took a back seat to other, seemingly more immediate concerns, such as building enough classrooms to house burgeoning enrollments and publishing manuscripts so as not to perish. Socialization was also deemed unimportant because of a pervasive assumption during this heyday of American higher education (the late 1960s and early 1970s) that new faculty members should continue in the tradition of their own graduate mentors. They needed no orientation by faculty at their new institutions because they were hired in large part to emulate the style and priorities of faculty at the prestigious institutions from which they graduated. Today, we are all too painfully aware that this traditional, collegial model is often inappropriate and that new faculty must often break away from what they observed or were taught in the research universities from which they graduated. They must instead learn about teaching, conducting research and scholarship, and performing institutional functions in a college or university with a quite different tradition, purpose, and culture. They need mentors who know the institution and can guide them to an appropriate style and set of priorities.

Senior faculty mentors can fill an important role by running interference, formulating supportive policies, providing encouragement, or serving as the friendly critic for new faculty members. It is essential that senior faculty help to establish and maintain an environment that is conducive to the professional growth of new faculty. More than anything else, successful mentors create conditions for taking risks and learning in the organizations that they lead. Successful mentoring can also fundamentally alter the culture and priorities of the institution: "Engaging senior faculty, who control the [reward] structure, in reflection on how excellent teaching is best supported can fundamentally alter institutional priorities toward a more appropriate balance between teaching and research—toward a better teaching environment" (Finkelstein and LaCelle-Peterson 1993, p. 2). A similar case could no doubt be made for a mentoring program that emphasizes research or scholarship, or service to the institution or local community. Senior faculty have played a major role in forging and sustaining the culture of their institutions. They also can play a major role in altering this culture.

Early retirement
The issue of early retirement is rather confusing. On the one

hand, there seems to be an abundance of senior faculty members at the present time who are receiving high salaries and by at least some accounts are less productive or competent than they once were (or at least less productive and competent than their younger colleagues). If this is the case, one cannot help but come to the conclusion that senior faculty members should be encouraged to retire early, thereby making room for more new faculty members, who will enter at lower salaries and make a greater contribution to the institution. Many respected observers of contemporary higher education have reached just such a conclusion. For instance, having reviewed much of the literature on faculty supply and demand in higher education, a group of scholars on faculty issues brought together by the Western Interstate Commission for Higher Education concluded that "institutional policies should provide opportunities for early retirement and for career-change training programs" (Gill et al. 1992, p. 7).

Conversely, much could be lost if many senior faculty members opt for early retirement. "Many senior faculty have the capacity to make continuing contributions" to their institutions, and "those who can enthusiastically deliver quality instruction and use their depth of experience to benefit students should be permitted to do so" (Lorenzo and Banach 1992, p. 12). Unfortunately, some of the very best faculty may be those most attracted to early retirement, precisely because they are likely to perceive themselves as having more options than those faculty members who are stagnant and fearful of starting a new career. Further, the push for early retirement may signal a lack of respect for those senior faculty who have made and continue to make significant contributions to the college or university.

Finally, senior faculty can play an invaluable service in orienting the new faculty to their profession and the institution. If many senior faculty take early retirement, then who will be available to ensure that the mission, values, and traditions of the academy will be sustained? Without a gradual transition from the old to the young faculty, some valuable lessons from the past will be lost, and the wheel is likely to be frequently and painfully reinvented by a young faculty starting from scratch.

Thus, early retirement involves a major dilemma. Although new faculty must be brought in to keep costs down and to respond to students' changing needs and rapidly shifting bases of knowledge, early retirement may lead to the loss of a college's or university's best senior faculty and to the retention of those senior faculty who should move on for the sake of their own stagnated lives as well as for the well-being of the institution.

Moreover, early retirement sends a message of disrespect that can adversely affect the morale and productivity of *all* senior faculty members, regardless of their sense of generativity. As one senior faculty member we know recently observed, "It is hard living with the fact that the most valuable contribution I can make to this institution at this point in my career is to retire and open a position for someone who is younger and more enthusiastic." This is indeed a sad state of affairs if, after a lifetime of service to his college, the only contribution he can make is to leave.

Career alternatives

Early retirement is at best a stopgap. It creates "flexibility only slightly sooner than would have occurred anyway during the critical period of the years 1985 to 2000" (Renner 1986, p. 312). The goal should be not to get rid of a large number of senior faculty, but "to more evenly distribute faculty ages and to allow the expansion [in student enrollments] predicted to begin in the year 2000 to more fully support its true costs" (p. 312). The replacement of many senior faculty with junior faculty would be moreover a "false economy": "It would begin again another cycle that would be difficult to support later" (p. 312), that is, another crisis in the faculty cohort when all of these young faculty hired in the year 2000 are ready to retire in 2035.

Suggesting that early retirement will not solve the problem and that other options must be considered to address the challenges associated with a very large faculty cohort is quite prophetic. In many instances, senior faculty can be replaced with part-time or adjunct faculty, thereby achieving a "real" economy. But for this proposal to work, colleges and universities must encourage faculty to consider shifting their careers in midlife. Though Renner does not primarily concern himself with describing what such a program might look like, he does address several of the major concerns with this strategy.

First, evidence from a research project at Dalhousie University in Canada indicates that about 40 percent of its faculty would be interested in an alternative career. Further, those who expressed interest are more likely to feel trapped in their profession than those who did not, thus suggesting that such a program is most likely to attract faculty who are most burned out.

Moreover, the professional productivity of these two groups is about the same, although those who want to consider an alternative are more interested in teaching than research and have fewer publications and research grants to their credit than those who are not interested in this option. Thus, an alternative career will not necessarily take away the best and the brightest of the faculty:

> *There is no reason to believe that a Career Alternatives program would selectively cost a university its best people. On the contrary, those who expressed an interest in a Career Alternative represented a cross-section of the faculty on professional and demographic variables. They differed from those who were not interested in a Career Alternative only on their current level of personal dissatisfaction with their work. . . . There appears to be a group of faculty who would like to step aside, if that were made financially feasible, thus making room for new young faculty* (Renner 1991, p. 122).

Yet this same argument could be made for the value of an early retirement plan, as such a program would also allow faculty to move on to a second career or pursue a more gratifying avocational interest. Moreover, if similar results were obtained in other colleges and universities that are less oriented toward research, one wonders whether it is a good idea to lose those faculty who are most interested in teaching and retain those who are most interested in research. An orientation toward teaching may be particularly important as contemporary colleges and universities face tighter budgets and a greater demand for accountability from the public with regard to quality of education.

What specifically can be done to encourage senior faculty in their exploration of alternative careers?

> *There are some [senior faculty] for whom the whole direction of career needs to be rethought. This is ex-*

ceedingly difficult for faculty and other professionals. Institutions and colleges could be more active in supporting individuals seeking out new directions of work. Leaves of absence to test out new jobs and support for retraining are two of the institutional means available. Disciplinary groups could be more supportive than they often are of members who change careers. But it is, of course, individuals who need the courage to embark on such changes. Perhaps, if there were more information available that would encourage people to seek such possibilities and see them as promising of success, they would be more frequently undertaken (Corcoran and Clark 1985, p. 75).

In most instances, neither early retirement programs nor alternative careers should be considered until a faculty member has availed himself or herself of some form of life or career counseling. Conversely, a life- or career-counseling program should be planned in conjunction with institutional initiatives that identify potential options for a career, both inside and outside the academy, for those faculty members who are "loosened up" by the planning process.

Linking faculty evaluation and development

"Academic evaluation systems need to be part of a professional development program and should be sufficiently flexible to accommodate changing patterns and levels of faculty productivity. Posttenure reviews should be structured as part of a faculty professional development program" (Gill et al. 1992, p. 7). In other words, we should not evaluate what we cannot develop (Bergquist 1981; Bergquist and Phillips 1975a, 1977). This is particularly the case for senior faculty, who usually already have tenure and have achieved the highest academic position in their institutions. Not only do senior faculty not appreciate the paperwork and administrative hassles of post-tenure review, they also are inclined to interpret this review as a sign that their contributions are not appreciated or that their continuing ability to serve their institution is being questioned.

Yet if evaluation is coupled with a professional development program or, even more specifically, a professional plan, then it holds the potential that senior faculty will receive it in a positive manner. "Institutions have much invested in their tenured faculty. For some institutions, post-tenure evaluation tied to faculty development may be but one way to protect and renew a critical human resource—the resource that directly helps shape institutional flexibility and quality. And therein lies the opportunity" (Licata 1986, p. 69).

Colleges and universities may find a few senior faculty members who are simply performing below par or who find themselves in especially unproductive situations for various reasons. Departmental, collegiate, and institutional leaders should help improve, reassign, retrain, or outplace faculty members or administrators who are no longer productive or who can no longer thrive in their current situations.

Proactive arrangement of opportunities for development

This monograph has consistently referred to authors who have found it is essential that faculty not become stuck or disillusioned. This situation can threaten vitality anytime, but it is particularly a problem for senior faculty who do not have the automatic mechanisms for support and feedback found in pretenure years or the options they used to have. Thus, institutions should identify, develop, and support numerous opportunities for faculty to enrich their work, such as sabbaticals, team teaching, fellowships, part-time administration, employee "loan programs" with other organizations, faculty exchange programs with other institutions, and so on. And administrators should proactively encourage faculty to participate in these opportunities.

Faculty renewal in content and technical skills

The task of staying up to date in one's field is becoming increasingly difficult. The growth rate of knowledge is phenomenal: Each year the Institute of Scientific Information processes 7,000 different journals with 2,500 issues, 4,200 articles, and 3,800 references, and each year 80,000 sources publish over 2 million papers (Dubin 1990). Scientific and technical information is doubling every five to seven years (Naisbett 1982). And the acquisition of new knowledge is made more complex because many new findings are made at the intersection of disciplines, requiring one to be both a specialist and a generalist.

New technology is exhibiting parallel growth, and professionals are faced with an enormous explosion in knowledge and technology. "Unfortunately, obsolescence is almost inevitable unless positive efforts are made to counteract it. . . . Overcoming or staving off obsolescence is not an easy matter. It requires some fundamental changes in habits, strong personal motivation, and supportive conditions in the workplace" (Dubin 1990, pp. 10–11). Because of the enormity of the problem of staying up to date, the shift in responsibility for deepening oneself technically and cognitively has gone from being an individual's problem to also becoming the organization's problem. Exemplary companies in the United States such as the Malcolm Baldrige winners and innovative companies such as the Saturn Corporation, for example, have begun to require employees to spend significant work time on continuing education, and to provide specialized training and other activities and resources, such as conferences and easy access to computerized literature bases.

At the same time, special conditions and characteristics of higher education exacerbate the problem of obsolescence. Unfortunately, these conditions are well known to academicians: Public financial support has drastically declined for many institutions, institutions have cut faculty and support staff and asked the remaining demoralized faculty to carry heavier loads, opportunities for advancement by moving to new institutions are greatly reduced, faculty are teaching with obsolete equipment, fewer sabbaticals are available, money is not available for conferences, and the public is asking faculty to spend more time teaching while at the same time looking to their research to fuel the engine of the economy. In response to these conditions, colleges and universities are redesigning themselves and expecting faculty to make these new designs a reality.

Specifically with regard to senior faculty, traditional characteristics of higher education also contribute to the problem of obsolescence. Typically, new faculty automatically find themselves in a tenure-track system that expects and rewards them for performing at the top of their field. Mid-career faculty (often full professors), on the other hand, seldom have a systematic reward structure to motivate them to stay up to date. Colleges and universities need to provide specific mechanisms and programs that both support and ensure continual updating in content and technical knowledge. The institution can no longer expect the faculty member to address this area alone.

Development for administrators

Without question, administrators are one of the most important keys to individual and institutional vitality. They control or influence nearly all the individual and institutional features that affect productivity. But the people who take on this crucial role and who themselves are frequently senior faculty seldom have formal training in monitoring or facilitating individual or institutional productivity.

In addition, administrators, especially department chairs and heads, are being asked to take on more and more new, diverse, and critical responsibilities under conditions of declining public support and increasing public scrutiny—28 roles for a department head (researcher, mentor, planner, for example) according to one count (Tucker 1984) and 97 activities for a department chair according to another (Creswell et al. 1990). But formal training is seldom available for these roles or activities.

To achieve faculty development and institutional productivity, we should perhaps focus on the development of administrators.

Not surprisingly, many writers suggest that to achieve faculty development and institutional productivity, we should perhaps focus on the development of administrators, that is, on department heads, deans, directors, provosts, and so on (Miller 1990). Effective and extensive administrative development programs increase the competency of campus leaders in their work, enable leaders to knowledgeably monitor and facilitate faculty and institutional productivity, and allow them to practice what they preach by engaging in their own development while encouraging the development of their faculty colleagues.

Conclusions

This monograph has identified the immense changes in higher education our faculty are expected to accomplish in the next decades, the exploding knowledge and technology base that constantly threatens to make them out of date, the fact that the majority of our faculty will be in their 50s or early 60s and the special benefits and challenges that situation presents, the individual, institutional, and leadership factors found to affect vitality, and ways to ensure a continually competent and productive faculty and organization. While we hope to have brought this information together in a useful form and added some new insights—especially on adult and career development—much of this information is not new.

There is no shortage of ideas about the characteristics of the aging faculty or strategies for helping faculty and higher education organizations remain vital (see, e.g., Baldwin, Brakeman, and Edgerton 1981; Bland and Schmitz 1990; Horner, Murray, and Rushton 1989; Schuster and Wheeler 1990; Wulff and Nyquist 1993). And the individual and institutional factors associated with faculty productivity have been described before. It is puzzling, then, why so few institutions actually invest significantly, either intellectually or financially, in these efforts to make faculty more motivated and the setting more conducive to productivity. Although about 1 percent of the academic budget should be spent on faculty development (Bevan 1985) and exemplary corporations claim to spend much more, few higher education institutions invest heavily in or take an informed, purposeful systems approach to maintaining the productivity of their faculty members.

We believe one reason is the previous lack of a clear profile of the features that affect senior faculty members' productivity and vitality. Without this information, leaders have not known where to invest resources and thus perhaps been reticent to do so. It is hoped this monograph will overcome this barrier. We must take steps to fully engage and ensure the competence and vitality of all our faculty members, the majority of whom are now "senior." We must monitor the individual, institutional, and leadership factors that facilitate vitality. We must address weaknesses in these factors through a comprehensive approach and encourage administrators to use such a comprehensive approach to address faculty and institutional development, which would include training on such things as features of productive faculty members and effective academic organizations. In addition, we must continually evaluate each part of the comprehensive approach. This information would serve as the basis for constantly improving and tailoring the approach to one's institution. It would also document for all stakeholders the benefits of investing in the development of faculty and administrators.

Let us return to the questions posed at the beginning of this monograph. Is the fact that 50 percent of our full-time faculty will soon be over 55 cause for alarm? Or are we fortunate to be undertaking major changes in higher education just when we have our most experienced faculty members on board? Just because there is snow on the roof, should we assume that the fire in the furnace has gone out? Our review of the literature suggests that senior faculty members are perhaps most interesting and capable people at this point in their lives. The fire still burns brightly and with considerable warmth. Senior faculty still question and probe but with new purpose and commitment. These men and women have

much to contribute to our society and, in particular, to our colleges and universities. Whether they are still vital, or can once again be vital, largely depends on the organization. Our collegiate institutions and "graying" faculty like Stephen Abbot who have effectively served these institutions for many years certainly deserve this attention. More pragmatically, they require this attention if colleges and universities are to be successfully redesigned to meet the challenges and needs of the 21st century.

APPENDIX: Critical Reflections on the Studies Cited in This Monograph

This monograph has been prepared specifically for those leaders of collegiate institutions who must address the issue of vitality among senior faculty in the decisions they make and the ways they relate to these seasoned members of their faculty. We have therefore chosen not to engage many of the controversies associated with the research we have cited. Nevertheless, we would be irresponsible if we ignored these controversies and failed to bring them to the attention of those readers who want to explore the issues more deeply.

Specifically, the focus is on methodological problems that underlie some of the studies we have cited. Many of the studies cited offer generalizations about senior faculty that are based on data collected from a specific group of faculty members, but many of the other studies are based on comparisons drawn between faculty members (or, more generally, adults) of differing ages. Several problems are associated with both types of studies: the use of cross-sectional methodologies and retrospective reporting, and the failure to identify individual differences.

Cross-sectional studies. Ideally, we should be conducting longitudinal studies of faculty members, with these faculty members serving as their own "controls" when studying changes over time. We should be drawing comparisons between specific faculty members when they are young and when they are old. Instead, we tend to use cross-sectional methods, comparing one group of young faculty members with a second group of older faculty members. When a cross-sectional approach is used, we can never be confident that the differences we observe are a function of age or of some other confounding variable, such as differences in the historical events that have affected these two cohorts.

Do we know, for example, whether faculty in their 50s or 60s differ from those in their 20s with regard to their attitudes about higher education as a result of different ages or the different status of America's colleges and universities in the 1960s and 1990s? More precisely, we may be observing a critical interaction between age and experience. A 28-year-old faculty member may experience the problems, challenges, and opportunities in contemporary colleges and universities quite differently from his or her 58-year-old colleagues. They may share the same experience but have different perceptions and interpretations of this experience. "Regardless of age, faculty who are hired around the same period of time are likely to hold similar views of their own academic setting, simply because they have been through some of the same experiences together" (D. Kelly 1991, p. 16).

The character of a specific institution might also change over time, leading to differences in faculty members' attitudes, regardless of age. A faculty member who applied for tenure when a college was still oriented toward teaching will have much more in common with another faculty member from that same era than a faculty member (of any age) who applied for tenure at a later date, when the college became oriented more toward research. Different organizational or societal expectations and pressures can dramatically shape the character of a faculty member's career and sense of self-worth and competence (Sheehy 1995).

The influence of specific events and historical periods in the lives of faculty members can be even more influential if they help to create self-fulfilling prophecies. If a faculty member—let's call her "Susan"—was expected to publish or perish as an assistant professor, then she is likely to define productivity and self-worth as an academician in terms of publishing rates and quality, even after she receives her promotions and tenure. We say that Susan is successful in her research-oriented university because her own criteria of success are compatible with those of her colleagues and the university as a whole. But Susan's criteria for success may have been forged primarily by her early experiences at the university, making the formation of these criteria a self-fulfilling prophecy.

The impact of the institution and its priorities on Susan are rarely discussed. Her research orientation is assumed to be part of her "personality" or "attitude" rather than a product of her environment. Thus, when Susan and colleagues of her era later confront a quite different environment at the university, which has a new emphasis on teaching and service, their reactions are likely to be interpreted as internal and related to age. Susan expresses her anger about the loss of support for research at the university and refers to the good old days when she had release time and travel money for conferences. Her younger colleagues and the administrators at her university write off her complaints as a sign of her midlife crisis, when in fact her discontent has more to do with the shift in priorities at her university.

The key to understanding what has happened with Susan and her senior colleagues lies in conducting longitudinal rather than cross-sectional studies. Unfortunately, longitudinal studies of faculty members have rarely been performed, and this dearth of such studies casts doubt on conclusions reached about shifts in faculty as a function of age. Because the data in most studies of the relationship between faculty careers and aging are cross-sectional rather than longitudinal, "there is little or no empirical evidence that changes in values and performance are age-related and recur across generations of professors" (Lawrence 1984, p. 57). Similarly, with a cross-sectional study, "it is important to recognize that particular historical events may account for some of the differences found. . . . An approaching tenure decision has different stressful consequences today than it did 20 years ago for a young assistant professor" (Baldwin and Blackburn 1981, p. 602). Moreover, for cross-sectional studies, "the cohort effect probably has an important impact on the findings. In other words, the faculty career pattern of someone who is 60 years old today may not necessarily be consistent with the experience of a 40-year-old faculty member 20 years from now" (D. Kelly 1991, p. 4).

Retrospective reporting. While many of the studies of change in abilities and attitudes among older adults—and specifically senior faculty—are based on cross-sectional comparisons, others are based on retrospective assessments by the people being studied. The person being interviewed or surveyed reflects on his or her life experiences and identifies changes that have occurred over time in their abilities and attitudes. Although the conclusions reached by these studies are of great value with regard to understanding how senior faculty perceive and interpret changes in their lives, these conclusions do not necessarily tell us much about the actual changes (if any) that occurred.

Based on results from one of the few longitudinal studies done of adults over a life span (Vaillant 1977), our experiences at any specific moment in our life often look quite different at the moment they occurred from what they do 10 or 20 years later when we are asked to reflect on them. We tend to impose order and coherence on events and life challenges many years later. The event or challenge was often experienced as much more chaotic and overwhelming when it actually occurred.

Thus, we must be cautious in accepting the conclusions of any retrospective study. The seeming order and predictability of crises and transitions in one's life may say more about how we recall and talk about our life experiences than about how we actually experience them firsthand. With specific regard to the studies of faculty vitality, we should be careful about uncritically accepting results from studies based primarily on the examination of differences as perceived by the faculty themselves between who they are now and who they think they were a certain number of years ago.

Failure to consider individual differences. It is always very tempting to draw general conclusions about senior faculty based on the results of several impressive national studies, especially if these studies are large, quantitative, and conducted by a major national association or research institute. We must be very cautious, however, given the significant differences that could be found among faculty as a function of gender, race, ethnicity, type of institution, discipline, level of success and satisfaction with one's career, socioeconomic level, and so on. The results of one study (Braskamp et al. 1982, p. 22) would suggest that we must be particularly careful in making generalizations about senior faculty, for individual differences among these men and women may be particularly pronounced. At this point in their careers, senior faculty have the greatest opportunity to branch out and to make a distinctive contribution to their disciplines, institutions, students, or avocations. They can finally begin to listen to those "voices from other rooms" that they ignored while establishing their careers, families, and personal identities.

What do we know about individual differences among senior faculty? The existing literature offers primarily cautionary notes rather than enlightening data. For instance:

> . . . the literature tends to make assumptions about faculty careers [that] are linked closely to age. Because the reports provided by the National Center [for] Education Statistics do not break down the data to indicate the relationship [among] age, gender, ethnicity, length of time as a faculty member, and academic rank, assumptions about faculty career patterns may not be accurate. . . . In reviewing the studies of faculty careers, it is important to separate age-related issues from career-development issues [that] may not be related to age (D. Kelly 1991, p. 4).

Similarly, senior faculty probably differ with regard to not only career stages, but also discipline, institutional type, gender, and ethnicity (Baldwin 1990).

Both Kelly and Baldwin go one step farther with regard to the influence of gender by citing research regarding the greater complexity of careers for women than men and many women's greater need for flexibility in balancing work and family. Baldwin does not speculate, however, about how these differences might specifically play out with regard to faculty careers. Although Kelly cites many studies that identify major differences between male and female faculty members, she does not identify any that specifically address gender differences among senior faculty. She does offer the very telling point, however, that women often move more slowly up the academic ladder than men, take time off from their jobs to raise a family, or enter the faculty ranks at a later age. Thus, differences between male and female faculty in their 50s may be attributed to differences in career stage rather than gender per se.

One might similarly wonder about the confounding of such variables as race, ethnicity, discipline, and institutional type with age, career stage, and gender. To what extent are certain racial and ethnic minority faculty similar to female faculty in that they are likely to move more slowly up the ranks or enter the academic ranks later in life? Are faculty in certain disciplines (e.g., history, philosophy, or sociology) more likely to feel trapped in their academic professions than are faculty in other disciplines or professions (e.g., engineering or medicine)? What about differences in the perceptions of institutional leaders among senior faculty in community colleges (who are often among the founders of their institutions) compared to those from four-year universities that were founded many years ago? We clearly need more research that explores differences among senior faculty and examines the interdependence of demographic variables. Quantitative studies will tell us something about the magnitude of these differences and the scope of the interdependencies. Qualitative studies will inform us about the ways in which these individual differences influence faculty careers and faculty vitality.

We also need studies of individual differences that focus not on these demographic differences (input measures) but rather on differences in outcomes among senior faculty (output measures). Rather than just beginning with individual differences and tracing their impact on faculty, we must begin with faculty who have arrived at different places in their academic careers and then trace the causes of these differences. One of the few studies that compared senior faculty who differ from one another specifically with regard to outcomes investigated differences between faculty who were designated by their department chairs as middle-aged and disillusioned and faculty who were also middle-aged but exemplary performers (Boice 1993, pp. 34, 36). The rich insights this study offers regarding the causes of faculty burnout and the potential strategies to avoid or ameliorate this condition speak to the value of this approach and to the need for more studies of different groups of senior faculty.

Given that researchers in American higher education have just begun to study faculty at different ages, we cannot fault them for failing to conduct studies of individual differences among various groups of faculty with regard to changes in abilities and attitudes over time. Yet until these studies are conducted, we must be careful about generalizing the results already reported or prematurely basing strategies for revitalization on very general results.

REFERENCES

The Educational Resources Information Center (ERIC) Clearing-house on Higher Education abstracts and indexes the current litera-ture on higher education for inclusion in ERIC's database and an-nouncement in ERIC's monthly bibliographic journal, *Resources in Education* (RIE). Most of these publications are available through the ERIC Document Reproduction Service (EDRS). For publications cited in this bibliography that are available from EDRS, ordering number and price code are included. Readers who wish to order a publication should write to the ERIC Document Reproduction Service, 7420 Fullerton Road, Suite 110, Springfield, Virginia 22153-2852. (Phone orders with VISA or MasterCard are taken at 800/443-ERIC or 703/440-1400.) When ordering, please specify the docu-ment (ED) number. Documents are available as noted in micro-fiche (MF) and paper copy (PC). If you have the price code ready when you call, EDRS can quote an exact price. The last page of the latest issue of *Resources in Education* also has the current cost, listed by code.

Andrews, F.M., ed. 1979. *Scientific Productivity: The Effectiveness of Research Groups in Six Countries.* Cambridge, Eng.: Cambridge Univ. Press.

Aran, L., and J. Ben-David. 1968. "Socialization and Career Patterns as Determinants of Productivity of Medical Researchers." *Journal of Health and Social Behavior* 9: 13–15.

Argyris, C. 1968. "On the Effectiveness of Research and Develop-ment Organizations." *American Scientist* 56: 344–55.

Armour, R., et al. 1990. "Senior Faculty Careers and Personal De-velopment: A Survey." Paper presented at the 1989 Annual Meeting of the American Educational Research Association, March 27–31, San Francisco, California. ED 323 904. 31 pp. MF–01; PC–02.

Austin, A.E., and Z.F. Gamson. 1983. *Academic Workplace: New Demands, Heightened Tensions.* ASHE-ERIC Higher Education Report No. 10. Washington, D.C.: Association for the Study of Higher Education. ED 243 397. 131 pp. MF–01; PC–06.

Axelrod, J. 1973. *The University Teacher as Artist.* San Francisco: Jossey-Bass.

———. 1980. "From Counterculture to Counterrevolution: A Teaching Career." In *Improving Teaching Styles,* edited by K. Eble. New Directions for Teaching and Learning No. 8. San Francisco: Jossey-Bass.

Bagenstos, N.T. 1988. "Preparing Minorities and Women as Re-searchers: Have We Learned Anything?" Paper presented at the 1988 Annual Meeting of the American Educational Research Association, April, New Orleans, Louisiana. ED 294 469. 7 pp. MF–01; PC–01.

Baird, L. 1986. "What Characterizes a Productive Research Department?" *Research in Higher Education* 25(3): 211–25.

Baldwin, R.G. 1979. "Adult and Career Development: What Are the Implications for Faculty?" *Current Issues in Higher Education* No. 2: 13–20. ED 217 780. 114 pp. MF–01; PC not available EDRS.

———. 1984. "The Changing Development Needs of an Aging Professoriate." In *Teaching and Aging,* edited by C.M.N. Mehrotra. New Directions for Teaching and Learning No. 19. San Francisco: Jossey-Bass.

———. 1990. "Faculty Career Stages and Implications for Faculty Development." In *Enhancing Faculty Careers: Strategies for Development and Renewal,* edited by J.H. Schuster and D.W. Wheeler. San Francisco: Jossey-Bass.

———, ed. 1985. *Incentives for Faculty Vitality.* New Directions for Higher Education No. 51. San Francisco: Jossey-Bass.

Baldwin, R.G., and R.T. Blackburn. 1981. "The Academic Career as a Developmental Process: Implications for Higher Education." *Journal of Higher Education* 52(6): 598–614.

Baldwin, R., L. Brakeman, and R. Edgerton. 1981. *Expanding Faculty Options: Career Development Projects at Colleges and Universities.* Washington, D.C.: American Association for Higher Education.

Barley, Z.A., and B.K. Reman. 1979. "Faculty Role Development in University Schools of Nursing." *Journal of Nursing Administration* 9: 43–47.

Bean, J.P. 1982. "A Causal Model of Faculty Research Productivity." Paper presented at the 1982 Annual Meeting of the American Educational Research Association, March 19–23, New York, New York. ED 216 661. 33 pp. MF–01; PC–02.

Belenky, M., et al. 1986. *Women's Ways of Knowing.* New York: Basic Books.

Bensimon, E.M., A. Neumann, and R. Birnbaum. 1989. *Making Sense of Administrative Leadership: The 'L' Word in Higher Education.* ASHE-ERIC Higher Education Report No. 1. Washington, D.C.: George Washington Univ., Graduate School of Education and Human Development. ED 316 074. 121 pp. MF–01; PC–05.

Bergquist, W.H. 1981. *A Handbook of Faculty Development.* Vol. 3. Washington, D.C.: Council of Independent Colleges. ED 209 201. 360 pp. MF–01; PC not available EDRS.

———. 1993a. *The Four Cultures of the Academy.* San Francisco: Jossey-Bass.

———. 1993b. *The Postmodern Organization: Mastering the Art of Irreversible Change.* San Francisco: Jossey-Bass.

———. 1995. *Quality through Access: Access with Quality.* San Francisco: Jossey-Bass.

Bergquist, W.H., E.M. Greenburg, and G.A. Klaum. 1993. *In Our*

Fifties: Voices of Men and Women Reinventing Their Lives. San Francisco: Jossey-Bass.

Bergquist, W.H., and S.R. Phillips. 1975a. "Components of an Effective Faculty Development Program." *Journal of Higher Education* 16: 177–209.

————. 1975b. *A Handbook for Faculty Development,* edited by G.H. Quehl. Washington, D.C.: Council for the Advancement of Small Colleges. ED 115 174. 299 pp. MF–01; PC–12.

————. 1977. *A Handbook for Faculty Development,* edited by G.H. Quehl. Vol. 2. Washington, D.C.: Council for the Advancement of Small Colleges. ED 148 204. 323 pp. MF–01; PC not available EDRS.

Bergquist, W., S. Phillips, and S. Gruber. 1992. *Developing Human and Organizational Resources: A Comprehensive Manual.* San Francisco: Professional School of Psychology.

Bergquist, W., and B. Weiss. 1994. *Freedom! Narratives of Change in Hungary and Estonia.* San Francisco: Jossey-Bass.

Bevan, J.M. 1985. "Who Has the Role of Building Incentives?" In *Incentives for Faculty Vitality,* edited by R.G. Baldwin. New Directions for Higher Education No. 51. San Francisco: Jossey-Bass.

Biglan, A. 1996. "Relationships between Subject Matter Characteristics and the Structure and Output of University Departments." *Journal of Applied Psychology* 57(3): 204–13.

Birnbaum, P.H. 1983. "Predictors of Long-Term Research Performance." In *Managing Interdisciplinary Research,* edited by S.R. Epton, R.L. Payne, and A.W. Pearson. New York: John Wiley & Sons.

Blackburn, R.T. 1974. "The Meaning of Work in Academia." In *Assessing Faculty Effort,* edited by J.I. Doi. New Directions for Institutional Research No. 2. San Francisco: Jossey-Bass.

————. 1979. "Academic Careers: Patterns and Possibilities." *Current Issues in Higher Education* 2: 25–27.

Blackburn, R.T., C.E. Behymer, and D.E. Hall. 1978. "Research Note: Correlates of Faculty Publications." *Sociology of Education* 51: 132–41.

Blackburn, R.T., and J.H. Lawrence. 1986. "Aging and the Quality of Faculty Job Performance." *Review of Educational Research* 23(3): 265–90.

Blackburn, R.T., and J.A. Pitney. 1988. *Performance Appraisal for Faculty: Implications for Higher Education.* Technical Report No. 88-D-002.0. Ann Arbor, Mich.: National Center for Research to Improve Postsecondary Teaching and Learning. ED 316 066. 59 pp. MF–01; PC–03.

Bland, C.J. June 1997. "Beyond Corporate Downsizing: A Better Way for Medical Schools to Succeed in a Changing World."

Academic Medicine 72(6): 13–19.

Bland, C.J., S.N. Chou, and T.L. Schwenk. 1993. "The Productive Organization." In *Managing in Academics: A Health Center Model,* edited by J. Ridky and G.F. Sheldon. St. Louis: Quality Medical Publishing.

Bland, C.J., M.A. Hitchcock, W.A. Anderson, and F.T. Stritter. 1987. "Faculty Development Fellowship Programs in Family Medicine." *Journal of Medical Education* 62: 632–41.

Bland, C.J., and R.L. Holloway. 1995. "A Crisis of Mission: Faculty Roles and Rewards in an Era of Health-Care Reform." *Change* 27(5): 30–35.

Bland, C.J., and J. Ridky. 1993. "Human and Organizational Resource Development." In *Managing in Academics: A Health Center Model,* edited by J. Ridky and G.F. Sheldon. St. Louis: Quality Medical Publishing.

Bland, C.J., and M.T. Ruffin IV. 1992. "Characteristics of a Productive Research Environment: Literature Review." *Academic Medicine* 67: 385–97.

Bland, C.J., and C.C. Schmitz. 1986. "Characteristics of the Successful Researcher and Implications for Faculty Development." *Journal of Medical Education* 61: 22–31.

———. 1988. "Faculty Vitality on Review: Retrospect and Prospect." *Journal of Higher Education* 59(2): 190–224.

———. 1990. "An Overview of Research on Faculty and Institutional Vitality." In *Enhancing Faculty Careers: Strategies for Development and Renewal,* edited by J.H. Schuster and D.W. Wheeler. San Francisco: Jossey-Bass.

Blau, J.R. 1976. "Scientific Recognition: Academic Context in Professional Role." *Social Studies of Science* 6: 533–45.

Boice, R. 1986. "Faculty Development via Field Programs for Middle-Aged, Disillusioned Faculty." *Research in Higher Education* 25(2): 115–35.

———. 1992. *The New Faculty Member: Supporting and Fostering Professional Development.* San Francisco: Jossey-Bass.

———. 1993. "Primal Origins and Later Correctives for Midcareer Disillusionment." In *Developing Senior Faculty as Teachers,* edited by M. Stein and M. LaCelle-Peterson. New Directions for Teaching and Learning No. 55. San Francisco: Jossey-Bass.

Bowen, H.R., and J.H. Schuster. 1986. *American Professors: A National Resource Imperiled.* New York: Oxford Univ. Press.

Braskamp, L.A., et al. 1982. "Faculty Development and Achievement: A Faculty's View." Paper presented at the 1982 Annual Meeting of the American Educational Research Association, New York, New York.

Bray, D.W., and A. Howard. 1983. "The AT&T Longitudinal Studies of Managers." In *Longitudinal Studies of Adult Psychological*

Development, edited by K.W. Schaie. New York: Guilford Press.

Breneman, D.W. 1993. *Higher Education: On a Collision Course with New Realities.* Boston: American Student Assistance Corporation. ED 379 975. 33 pp. MF–01; PC–02.

Brief, A.P. 1984. *Productivity Research in the Behavioral and Social Sciences.* New York: Praeger.

Caffarella, R.S., R.A. Armour, B.S. Fuhrmann, and J.F. Wergin. 1989. "Midcareer Faculty: Refocusing the Perspective." *Review of Higher Education* 12(4): 403–10.

Cameron, K.S., and M. Tschirhart. 1992. "Postindustrial Environments and Organizational Effectiveness in Colleges and Universities." *Journal of Higher Education* 63(1): 86–108.

Carnegie Foundation for the Advancement of Teaching. 1985. "The Faculty: Deeply Troubled." *Change* 17(4): 31–34.

———. 1989. *The Condition of the Professoriate: Attitudes and Trends. A Technical Report.* Princeton, N.J.: Author. ED 312 963. 162 pp. MF–01; PC not available EDRS.

Cascio, W.F. 1993. "Downsizing: What Do We Know? What Have We Learned?" *Academy of Management Executives* 7: 95–104.

Cascio, W.F., and J.R. Morris. 1996a. "The Impact of Downsizing on the Financial Performance of Firms: 311 Firms That Downsized by 3% between 1980–1990." Faculty Working Paper Series. Denver: Univ. of Colorado, College of Business and Business Administration and Graduate School of Business Administration.

———. 1996b. "The Impact of Downsizing on the Financial Performance of Firms: 25 Downsized Firms Compared to Companies in the Same Industries." Faculty Working Paper Series. Denver: Univ. of Colorado, College of Business and Business Administration and Graduate School of Business Administration.

Clark, S.M. 1992. "Faculty Vitality." In *The Encyclopedia of Higher Education,* edited by B.R. Clark and G.R. Neave. Oxford, Eng.: Pergamon Press.

Clark, S.M., and M. Corcoran. 1985. "Individual and Organizational Contributions to Faculty Vitality: An Institutional Case Study." In *Faculty Vitality and Institutional Productivity: Critical Perspectives for Higher Education,* edited by S.M. Clark and D.R. Lewis. New York: Teachers College Press.

Clark, S.M., and D.R. Lewis. 1985. "Implications for Institutional Response." In *Faculty Vitality and Institutional Productivity: Critical Perspectives for Higher Education,* edited by S.M. Clark and D.R. Lewis. New York: Teachers College Press.

Cole, S. 1979. "Age and Scientific Performance." *American Journal of Sociology* 84: 958–77.

Cole, S., and J. Cole. 1967. "Scientific Output and Recognition: A Study in the Operation of the Award System in Science." *American Sociological Review* 32: 377–90.

Collins, J.C., and J.I. Porras. 1994. *Built to Last: Successful Habits of Visionary Companies*. New York: Harper Collins.

Corcoran, M., and S.M. Clark. 1984. "Professional Socialization and Contemporary Career Attitudes of Three Faculty Generations." *Review of Higher Education* 30: 131–53.

———. 1985. "The 'Stuck' Professor: Insights into an Aspect of the Faculty Vitality Issue." In *The Professoriate: Occupation in Crisis*, edited by C. Watson. Toronto: Ontario Institute for Studies in Education.

Cornwell, C.D. 1974. "Statistical Treatment of Data from Student Teaching Evaluation Questionnaires." *Journal of Chemical Education* 51: 155–60.

Crawley, A.L. 1995. "Senior Faculty Renewal at Research Universities: Implications for Academic Policy Development." *Innovative Higher Education* 20(2): 71–94.

Creswell, J.W. 1985. *Faculty Research Performance: Lessons from the Sciences and Social Sciences*. ASHE-ERIC Higher Education Report No. 4. Washington, D.C.: Association for the Study of Higher Education. ED 267 677. 92 pp. MF–01; PC–04.

Creswell, J.W., and J.P. Bean. 1996. "Research Output, Socialization, and the Biglan Model." *Research in Higher Education* 15: 69–89.

Creswell, J.W., et al. 1990. *The Academic Chairperson's Handbook*. Lincoln: Univ. of Nebraska Press.

Cytrynbaum, S., S. Lee, and D. Wadner. 1982. "Faculty Development through the Life Course: Application of Recent Adult Development Theory and Research." *Journal of Instructional Development* 5: 11–22.

Dennis, W. 1956. "Age and Productivity among Scientists." *Science* 123: 724–25.

Dill, D.D. 1982. "The Management of Academic Culture: Notes on the Management of Meaning and Social Integration." *Higher Education* 11: 303–20.

———. 1985. "Theory versus Practice in the Staffing of R&D Laboratories." *R&D Management* 15: 227–41.

———. 1986a. "Local Barriers and Facilitators of Research." Paper presented at the 1986 Annual Meeting of the American Educational Research Association, April, San Francisco, California.

———. 1986b. "Research as a Scholarly Activity: Context and Culture." In *Measuring Faculty Research Performance*, edited by J.W. Creswell. New Directions for Institutional Research No. 50. New York: Jossey-Bass.

Drew, D.E. 1985. *Strengthening Academic Science*. New York: Praeger.

Driver, M. 1979. "Career Concept and Career Management in Organizations." In *Behavior Problems in Organizations*, edited by C.L. Cooper. Englewood Cliffs, N.J.: Prentice-Hall.

————. 1982. "Career Concepts: A New Approach to Career Research." In *Career Issues in Human Resources Management*, edited by R. Katz. Englewood Cliffs, N.J.: Prentice-Hall.

Dubin, S.S. 1990. "Maintaining Competence through Updating." In *Maintaining Professional Competence: Approaches to Career Enhancement, Vitality, and Success throughout a Work Life*, edited by S.L. Willis and S.S. Dubin. San Francisco: Jossey-Bass.

Eckert, R.E., and J.E. Stecklein. 1961. *Job Motivations and Satisfactions of College Teachers: A Study of Faculty Members in Minnesota Colleges*. Washington, D.C.: U.S. Government Printing Office.

Edwards, R. October 1994. "Toward Constructive Review of Disengaged Faculty." *AAHE Bulletin:* 6–7+.

El-Khawas, E. 1991. "Senior Faculty in Academe: Active, Committed to the Teaching Role." *Research Briefs* 2: 1–12. ED 381 104. 14 pp. MF–01; PC–01.

Epson, S.R., R.L. Payne, and A.W. Pearson. 1983. *Managing Interdisciplinary Research*. New York: John Wiley & Sons.

Erikson, E.H. 1982. *The Life Cycle Completed: A Review*. New York: W.W. Norton & Co.

————. 1985. *Childhood and Society*. 35th Anniversary Edition. New York: W.W. Norton & Co.

Farr, J.L., and C.L. Middlebrooks. 1990. "Enhancing Motivation to Participate in Professional Development." In *Maintaining Professional Competence: Approaches to Career Enhancement, Vitality, and Success throughout a Work Life*, edited by S.L. Willis and S.S. Dubin. San Francisco: Jossey-Bass.

Finkelstein, M.J. 1982. "Faculty Colleagueship Patterns and Research Productivity." Paper presented at the 1982 Annual Meeting of the American Educational Research Association, March, New York, New York. ED 216 633. 42 pp. MF–01; PC–02.

————. 1984. *The American Academic Profession*. Columbus: Ohio State Univ. Press.

————. 1996. "Faculty Vitality in Higher Education." In *Integrating Research on Faculty: Seeking New Ways to Communicate about the Academic Life of Faculty*. Conference Report: Results of a forum sponsored by the National Center for Education Statistics, the Association for Institutional Research, and the American Association of State Colleges and Universities, January 10–11, 1994, Washington, D.C. Washington, D.C.: National Center for Education Statistics.

Finkelstein, M.J., and M.W. LaCelle-Peterson, eds. 1993. *Developing Senior Faculty as Teachers*. New Directions for Teaching and Learning No. 55. San Francisco: Jossey-Bass.

Fox, M.F. 1991. "Gender, Environmental Milieu, and Productivity in Science." In *The Outer Circle: Women in the Scientific Com-*

munity, edited by H. Zuckerman, J.R. Cote, and J.T. Bruer. New York: W.W. Norton & Co.

Freedman, M. 1979. *Academic Culture and Faculty Development.* Berkeley, Calif.: Montaigne.

Furniss, W.T. 1981. *Reshaping Faculty Careers.* Washington, D.C.: American Council on Education.

Gardner, J.W. 1963. *Self-Renewal.* New York: Harper & Row.

Gill, J.I., et al. 1992. "Faculty Supply and Demand: Data Sources and Data Needs." *Research Dialogues* 32. ED 370 457. 10 pp. MF–01; PC–01.

Gilligan, C. 1982. *In a Different Voice.* Cambridge, Mass.: Harvard Univ. Press.

Gustad, J.W. 1960. *The Career Decisions of College Teachers.* College Park, Md.: U.S. Dept. of Health, Education, and Welfare.

Hargens, L.L. 1978. "Relations between Work Habits, Research Technologies, and Eminence in Science." *Sociology of Work and Work Occupations* 5: 97–112.

Havighurst, R.J. 1964. "Stages of Vocational Development." In *Man in a World of Work,* edited by H. Borow. Boston: Houghton Mifflin.

Heilman, J.D., and W.D. Armentrout. 1936. "The Ratings of College Teachers by Their Students." *Journal of Educational Psychology* 27: 197–216.

Hemphill, J.K. 1955. "Leadership Behavior Associated with the Administrative Reputation of College Departments." *Educational Psychology* 46: 385–401.

Hitchcock, M.A., C.J. Bland, F.P. Hekelman, and M.G. Blumenthal. 1995. "Professional Networks: The Influence of Colleagues on the Academic Success of Faculty." *Academic Medicine* 70: 1108–16.

Hodgkinson, H.L. 1974. "Adult Development: Implications for Faculty and Administrators." *Educational Record* 55(4): 263–74.

Holland, J.L. 1985. *Making Vocational Choices: A Theory of Vocational Personalities and Work Environments.* Englewood Cliffs, N.J.: Prentice-Hall.

Horner, K.L., H.G. Murray, and J.P. Rushton. 1989. "Relation between Aging and Rated Teaching Effectiveness of Academic Psychologists." *Psychology and Aging* 4(2): 226–29.

Horner, K.L., J.P. Rushton, and P.A. Vernon. 1986. "Relation between Aging and Research Productivity of Academic Psychologists." *Psychology and Aging* 1(4): 319–24.

Hoyt, D.P., and R.K. Spangler. 1978. "Administrative Effectiveness of the Academic Department Head: Correlates of Effectiveness." Report No. 47. Manhattan: Kansas State Univ., Center for Faculty Evaluation and Development, Office of Educational Research. ED 171 215. 17 pp. MF–01; PC–01.

Inhelder, B., and J. Piaget. 1958. *The Growth of Logical Thinking from Childhood to Adolescence: An Essay on the Construction of Formal Operations Structures.* New York: Basic Books.

Johnston, R. 1994. "Effects of Resource Concentration on Research Performance." *Higher Education* 28: 25–37.

Jordan, J.M., M. Meador, and S. Walters. 1988. "Effects of Department Size and Organization on the Research Productivity of Academic Economists." *Economics of Education Review* 7: 251–55.

Kalivoda, P., G.R. Sorrell, and R.D. Simpson. 1994. "Nurturing Faculty Vitality by Matching Institutional Interventions with Career-Stage Needs." *Innovative Higher Education* 18: 255–72.

Kallio, R.E., and T.J. Ging. 1985. "The Effects of Aging on Faculty Productivity." Paper presented at the 1985 Annual Meeting of the Association for the Study of Higher Education, March 15–17, Chicago, Illinois. ED 259 628. 47 pp. MF–01; PC–02.

Kanter, R.M. 1977. *Men and Women of the Corporation.* New York: Basic Books.

———. 1979. "Changing the Shape of Work: Reform in Academe." *Current Issues in Higher Education* 1: 3–9.

Katz, R.L. 1978. "Job Longevity as a Situational Factor in Job Satisfaction." *Administrative Science Quarterly* 23: 204–23.

Kegan, R. 1982. *The Evolving Self: Problems and Process in Human Development.* Cambridge, Mass.: Harvard Univ. Press.

Kelly, D.K. 1991. *Linking Faculty Development with Adult Development: An Individualized Approach to Professional Growth and Renewal.* ED 337 103. 59 pp. MF–01; PC not available EDRS.

Kelly, M.E. 1986. "Enablers and Inhibitors to Research Productivity among High- and Low-Producing Vocational Educational Faculty Members." *Journal of Vocational Education Research* 11: 63–80.

Knight, W.H., and M.C. Holen. 1985. "Leadership and the Perceived Effectiveness of Department Chairpersons." *Journal of Higher Education* 56: 678–90.

Knorr, K., R. Mittermeir, G. Aichholzer, and C. Waller. 1979. "Individual Publication Productivity as a Social Position Effect in Academic and Industrial Research Units." In *Scientific Productivity: The Effectiveness of Research Groups in Six Countries,* edited by F.M. Andrews. Cambridge, Eng.: Cambridge Univ. Press.

LaCelle-Peterson, M.W., and M.J. Finkelstein. 1993. "Institutions Matter: Campus Teaching Environments' Impact on Senior Faculty." In *Developing Senior Faculty as Teachers,* edited by M.J. Finkelstein and M.W. LaCelle-Peterson. New Directions in Teaching and Learning No. 55. San Francisco: Jossey-Bass.

Latham, G.P., and T.R. Mitchell. 1976. *Behavioral Criteria and Potential Reinforcers for the Engineer/Scientist in an Industrial Setting.* Washington, D.C.: American Psychological Association.

Latham, G.P., and K.N. Wexley. 1981. *Increasing Productivity through Performance Appraisal.* Reading, Mass.: Addison-

Wesley.

Lawrence, J.H. 1984. "Faculty Aging and Teaching." In *Teaching and Aging,* edited by C.M. Mehrota. New Directions for Teaching and Learning No. 19. San Francisco: Jossey-Bass.

———. 1985. "Developmental Needs as Intrinsic Incentives." In *Incentives for Faculty Vitality,* edited by R.J. Baldwin. New Directions for Higher Education No. 51. San Francisco: Jossey-Bass.

Lawrence, J.H., and R.T. Blackburn. 1985. "Faculty Careers: Maturation, Demographic, and Historical Effects." *Research in Higher Education* 22(2): 135–54.

———. 1988. "Age as a Predictor of Faculty Productivity: Three Conceptual Approaches." *Journal of Higher Education* 59(1): 22–38.

Lehman, H.C. 1953. *Age and Achievement.* Princeton, N.J.: Princeton Univ. Press.

———. 1966. "The Psychologist's Most Creative Years." *American Psychologist* 21: 363–69.

Levine, A., et al. 1989. *Shaping Higher Education's Future: Demographic Realities and Opportunities, 1990–2000.* San Francisco: Jossey-Bass.

Levine, S.L. 1989. *Promoting Adult Growth in Schools: The Promise of Professional Development.* Boston: Allyn & Bacon.

Levinson, D.J. 1996. *The Seasons of a Woman's Life.* New York: Knopf.

Levinson, D.J., C.M. Darrow, E.B. Klein, M.H. Levinson, and B. McKee. 1976. "Periods in the Adult Development of Men: Ages 18–45." *Counseling Psychologist* 6(1): 21–25.

Levinson, D.J., et al. 1978. *The Seasons of a Man's Life.* New York: Knopf.

Lewis, D.R., and W.E. Becker, Jr. 1979. *Academic Rewards in Higher Education.* Cambridge, Mass.: Ballinger.

Licata, C.M. 1986. *Post-tenure Faculty Evaluation: Threat or Opportunity?* ASHE-ERIC Higher Education Report No. 1. Washington, D.C.: Association for the Study of Higher Education. ED 270 009. 118 pp. MF–01; PC–05.

Linsky, A.S., and M.A. Straus. 1975. "Student Evaluations, Research Productivity, and Eminence of College Faculty." *Journal of Higher Education* 59: 89–102.

Locke, E.A., N.W. Fitzpatrick, and F.M. White. 1983. "Job Satisfaction and Role Clarity among University and College Faculty." *Review of Higher Education* 6: 343–65.

Locke, E.A., and G.P. Latham. 1984. *Goal Setting: A Motivational Technique That Works!* Englewood Cliffs, N.J.: Prentice-Hall.

Loevinger, J. March 1966. "The Meaning and Measurement of Ego Development." *American Psychologist* 21: 195–206.

Loevinger, J., R. Wessler, and C. Redmore. 1970. *Measuring Ego*

Development. San Francisco: Jossey-Bass.

Long, J.S., and R. McGinnis. 1981. "Organizational Context and Scientific Productivity." *American Sociological Review* 46: 422–42.

Lorenzo, A.L., and W.J. Banach. 1992. "Critical Issues Facing America's Community Colleges." Warren, Mich.: Macomb Press. ED 351 046. 26 pp. MF–01; PC–02.

Lovett, C.M., et al. 1984. "Vitality without Mobility: The Faculty Opportunities Audit." Washington, D.C.: American Association for Higher Education, Task Force on Personal Growth. ED 249 909. 44 pp. MF–01; PC–02.

McCarthy, M.J. 1972. "Correlates of Effectiveness among Academic Department Heads." Ph.D. thesis, Kansas State Univ.

McGee, G.W., and R.C. Ford. 1987. "Faculty Research Productivity and Intention to Change Positions." *Review of Higher Education* 11: 1–16.

McKeachie, W.K. 1982. "Enhancing Productivity in Postsecondary Education." *Journal of Higher Education* 53(4): 460–64.

Manis, J.G. 1951. "Some Academic Influences upon Publication Productivity." *Social Forces* 29: 267–72.

Mann, M.P. 1987. "Developmental Models of Faculty Careers: A Critique of Research and Theory." In *To Improve the Academy: Resources for Student, Faculty, and Institutional Development.* Vol. 6. Stillwater, Okla.: New Forums Press. ED 344 539. 210 pp. MF–01; PC–09.

Mausch, M. 1985. "Vicious Circles Organizations." *Administrative Science Quarterly* 30: 14–33.

Meltzer, L. 1956. "Scientific Productivity in Organizational Settings." *Journal of Social Issues* 12: 32–40.

Miller, D.B. 1990. "Organizational, Environmental, and Work Design Strategies That Foster Competence." In *Maintaining Professional Competence: Approaches to Career Enhancement, Vitality, and Success throughout a Work Life,* edited by S.L. Willis and S.S. Dubin. San Francisco: Jossey-Bass.

Minckley, B.B., and S.N. Punk, eds. 1981. *Creating Research Environments in the 1980s.* Results of the Fifth Midwest Nursing Research Conference, April 13–14, Madison, Wisconsin. Indianapolis: Midwest Alliance in Nursing. ED 272 226. 58 pp. MF–01; PC–03.

Naisbett, J. 1982. *Megatrends: Ten New Directions Transforming Our Lives.* New York: Warner Books.

National Center for Education Statistics. 1990. *Faculty in Higher Education Institutions: 1988.* Washington, D.C.: U.S. Dept. of Education, Office of Educational Research and Improvement. ED 321 628. 209 pp. MF–01; PC–09.

———. 1993. "National Study of Postsecondary Faculty." Washington, D.C.: U.S. Dept. of Education, Office of Educational Research and Improvement. ED 375 792. 44 pp. MF–01; PC–02.

Okrasa, W. 1987. "Differences in Scientific Productivity of Research Units: Measurement and Analysis of Output Inequality." *Scientometrics* 12: 221–39.

Oromaner, M. 1977. "Professional Age and the Reception of Sociological Publications: A Test of the Zuckerman-Merton Hypothesis." *Social Studies of Science* 7: 381–88.

Over, R. 1982. "Does Research Productivity Decline with Age?" *Higher Education* 13: 511–20.

———. 1988. "Does Scholarly Impact Decline with Age?" *Scientometrics* 13: 207–15.

———. 1989. "Age and Scholarly Impact." *Psychology and Aging* 4(2): 222–25.

Patton, C.V. 1978. "Midcareer Change and Early Retirement." In *Evaluating Faculty Performance and Vitality,* edited by Wayne R. Kirschling. New Directions for Institutional Research No. 20. San Francisco: Jossey-Bass.

Pellino, F.R., et al. 1981. *Planning and Evaluating Professional Growth Programs for Faculty.* Monograph Series 14. Ann Arbor, Mich.: Center for the Study of Higher Education.

Pelz, D.C. 1967. "Some Social Factors Related to Performance in a Research Organization." *Administrative Science Quarterly* 11: 311–25.

Pelz, D.C., and F.M. Andrews. 1966. *Scientists in Organizations: Productive Climates for Research and Development.* New York: John Wiley & Sons.

Perkoff, G.T. 1986. "The Research Environment in Family Practice." *Journal of Family Practice* 21: 389–93.

Peters, T.J., and R.J. Waterman, Jr. 1988. *In Search of Excellence: Lessons from America's Best-Run Companies.* New York: Harper & Row.

Pietrofesa, J.J., and H. Splete. 1996. *Career Development: Theory and Research.* Rev. ed. New York: Grunge & Stratton.

Pineau, C., and C. Levy-Leboyer. 1983. "Managerial and Organizational Determinants of Efficiency in Biomedical Research Teams." In *Managing Interdisciplinary Research,* edited by S.R. Epton, R.L. Payne, and A.W. Pearson. New York: John Wiley & Sons.

Reichheld, F.F. 1996. *The Loyalty Effect: The Hidden Force behind Growth, Profits, and Lasting Value.* Boston: Bain & Co./Harvard Business School Press.

Renner, K.E. 1986. "Tenure, Retirement, and the Year 2000: The Issues of Flexibility and Dollars." *Research in Higher Education* 26: 307–15.

———. 1991. "A Survey Tool, Retrenchment Blues, and a Career

Alternatives Program." *Canadian Journal of Higher Education* 21: 115–23.

Reskin, B.F. 1977. "Scientific Productivity and the Reward Structure of Science." *American Sociological Review* 42: 491–504.

Rice, R.E., and A.K. Austin. March/April 1988. "High Faculty Morale: What Exemplary Colleges Do Right." *Change:* 50–58.

————. 1990. "Organizational Impacts on Faculty Morale and Motivation to Teach." In *How Administrators Can Improve Teaching: Moving from Talk to Action in Higher Education,* edited by P. Seldin. San Francisco: Jossey-Bass.

Rice, R.E., and M.J. Finkelstein. 1993. "The Senior Faculty: A Portrait and Literature Review." In *Developing Senior Faculty as Teachers,* edited by M.J. Finkelstein and M.W. LaCelle-Peterson. New Directions for Teaching and Learning No. 55. San Francisco: Jossey-Bass.

Rubin, L. 1976. *The Worlds of Pain: Life in a Working Class Family.* New York: Basic Books.

Sanford, N. 1980. *Learning after College.* Berkeley, Calif.: Montaigne Press.

Sarason, S.B. 1977. *Work, Aging, and Social Change.* New York: Free Press.

Schaie, K.W. 1983. "The Seattle Longitudinal Study: A 21-Year Exploration of Psychometric Intelligence in Adulthood." In *Longitudinal Studies of Adult Psychological Development,* edited by K.W. Schaie. New York: Guilford Press.

Schuster, J.H., and D.W. Wheeler, eds. 1990. *Enhancing Faculty Careers: Strategies for Development and Renewal.* San Francisco: Jossey-Bass.

Schweitzer, J.C. 1988. "Personal, Organizational, and Cultural Factors Affecting Scholarly Research among Mass Communication Faculty." Paper presented at the 71st Annual Meeting of the Association for Education in Journalism and Mass Communication, July 2–5, Portland, Oregon. ED 295 268. 17 pp. MF–01; PC–01.

Seagren, A.T., J.W. Creswell, and D.W. Wheeler. 1993. *The Department Chair: New Roles, Responsibilities, and Challenges.* ASHE-ERIC Higher Education Report No. 1. Washington, D.C.: George Washington Univ., Graduate School of Education and Human Development. ED 363 164. 129 pp. MF–01; PC–06.

Sheehy, G. 1995. *New Passages: Mapping Your Life across Time.* New York: Random House.

Siegler, I. 1983. "Psychological Aspects of the Duke Longitudinal Studies." In *Longitudinal Studies of Adult Psychological Development,* edited by K.W. Schaie. New York: Guilford Press.

Simonton, D.K. 1984. *Genius, Creativity, and Leadership: Histiometric Inquiries.* Cambridge, Mass.: Harvard Univ. Press.

————. 1985. "Quality, Quantity, and Age: The Careers of Ten Distinguished Psychologists." *International Journal of Aging and Human Development* (21): 241–54.

Simpson, R.D., and W.K. Jackson. 1990. "A Multidimensional Approach to Faculty Vitality." In *Enchancing Faculty Careers: Strategies for Development and Renewal,* edited by J.H. Schuster and D.W. Wheeler. San Francisco: Jossey-Bass.

Sindermann, C.J. 1985. *The Joy of Science: Excellence and Its Rewards.* New York: Plenum Press.

Skipper, C.E. 1976. "Personal Characteristics of Effective and Ineffective University Leaders." *College and University* 51: 138–41.

Smith, C.G. 1971. "Scientific Performance and the Composition of Research Teams." *Administrative Science Quarterly* 16(4): 486–96.

Smith, S.L., D.R. Baker, M.E. Campbell, and M.E. Cunningham. 1985. "An Exploration of the Factors Shaping the Scholarly Productivity of Social Work Academicians." *Journal of Social Service Research* 8: 81–99.

Srivastva, S., D.L. Cooperider, and Associates. 1990. *Appreciative Management Leadership: The Power of Positive Thought and Action in Organizations.* San Francisco: Jossey-Bass.

Staw, B.M., and L.L. Cummings, eds. 1988. *Research in Organizational Behavior: An Annual Series of Analytical Essays and Critical Reviews.* Vol. 10. Greenwich, Conn.: JAI Press.

Steiner, G. October 1989. "Books: An Examined Life." *The New Yorker* 65(36): 142–46.

————, ed. 1965. *The Creative Organization.* Chicago: Univ. of Chicago Press.

Stinchcombe, A.L. Winter 1966. "On Getting 'Hung-up' and Other Assorted Illnesses." *Johns Hopkins Magazine* 28: 25–30.

Super, D.E. 1957. *The Psychology of Careers.* New York: Harper & Row.

Super, D.E., et al. 1963. *Career Development: Self-Concept Theory. Essays in Vocational Development.* New York: College Examination Board.

Tierney, W. 1987. "Facts and Constructs: Defining Reality in Higher Education Organizations." *Review of Higher Education* 11(1): 61–73.

Tucker, A. 1984. *Chairing the Academic Department: Leadership among Peers.* New York: ACE/Macmillan.

Tucker, M.L. December 1990. "Relationship between Aging and Job Satisfaction for Humanities and Social Science Faculty in the Virginia Community College System." Research Report No. 8-90. Charlottesville, Va.: Piedmont Virginia Community College, Office of Institutional Research and Planning. ED 327 225. 32 pp. MF–01; PC–02.

Turney, J.R. 1974. "Activity, Outcomes, Expectancies, and Intrinsic Activity Value as Predictors of Several Motivational Indexes for Technical Professionals." *Organizational Behavior and Human Performance* 11: 65–82.

Updike, J. 1960. *Rabbit Run.* New York: Knopf.

———. 1971. *Rabbit Redux.* New York: Knopf.

———. 1990. *Rabbit at Rest.* New York: Knopf.

Vaillant, G. 1977. *Adaptation to Life.* New York: Little, Brown.

Visart, N. 1979. "Communication between and within Research Units." In *Scientific Productivity: The Effectiveness of Research Groups in Six Countries,* edited by F.M. Andrews. Cambridge, Eng.: Cambridge Univ. Press.

Votruba, J.C. 1990. "Strengthening Competence and Vitality in Professional Development." In *Maintaining Professional Competence: Approaches to Career Enhancement, Vitality, and Success throughout a Work Life,* edited by S.L. Willis and S.S. Dubin. San Francisco: Jossey-Bass.

Vroom, V.H. 1964. *Work and Motivation.* New York: John Wiley & Sons.

Watson, G., and L.H. Grossman. 1994. "Pursuing a Comprehensive Faculty Development Program: Making Fragmentation Work." *Journal of Counseling and Development* 72: 465–73.

Wergin, J.F. 1994. *The Collaborative Department: How Five Campuses Are Inching toward Cultures of Collective Responsibility.* Washington, D.C.: American Association for Higher Education.

Wheeler, B.J. 1990. "Mature and Aging Scholars: How Do They Stay Current?" Paper presented at the 1990 Annual Conference of the Professional and Organizational Development Network, November, Lake Tahoe, California.

Wheeler, D., and J. Creswell. 1985. "Developing Faculty as Researchers." Paper presented at the 1985 Annual Meeting of the Association for the Study of Higher Education, March 15–17, Chicago, Illinois. ED 259 649. 43 pp. MF–01; PC–02.

Wheeler, D.W., and J.H. Schuster. 1990. "Building Comprehensive Programs to Enhance Faculty Development." In *Enhancing Faculty Careers: Strategies for Development and Renewal,* edited by J.H. Schuster and D.W. Wheeler. San Francisco: Jossey-Bass.

Willis, S.L., and J.L. Tosti-Vasey. 1990. "How Adult Development, Intelligence, and Motivation Affect Competence." In *Maintaining Professional Competence: Approaches to Career Enhancement, Vitality, and Success throughout a Work Life,* edited by S.L. Willis and S.S. Dubin. San Francisco: Jossey-Bass.

Wispe, L.G. 1969. "The Bigger, the Better: Productivity, Size." *American Psychologist* 24: 662–68.

Wrightsman, L.S. 1988. *Personality Development in Adulthood.* Newbury Park, Calif.: Sage.

Wulff, D.H., and J.D. Nyquist, eds. 1993. *To Improve the Academy: Resources for Faculty, Instructional, and Organizational Development.* Vol. 12. Stillwater, Okla.: New Forums Press.

Zuckerman, H. 1977. *Scientific Elite: Nobel Laureates in the United States.* New York: Free Press.

INDEX

A

Abbot, Stephen

    altering view of college teacher (1969–1979), 16–19

    An Explosive Decade (1959–1969), 15–17

    focus on teaching literature, 15

    Late Years (1989–1999), 23–24

    Middle Years (1979–1989), 19–23

    need to look upon a student as a whole person, not merely as a "mind" to be trained, 16

    only published longitudinal case study of a single faculty member

    over a 40-year period, 25

    return to lack of interest in ideas of students, 21–22

    return to share "in-process" explorations with his students, 23

    shift from teaching subject to teaching students, 16

    student years at Chicago (1947–1959), 13–15

academic evaluation systems

    need to be part of a professional development program, 113

access without quality is not true access, 6

administrators

    development for, 116

adult development theory

    applied to faculty, 44–48

    faculty careers can also be understood in terms of, 65

    misapplication to faculty, 48–50

age

    discrimination negatively affects performance, 31

    significant variable for needs and interests, 39–40

alternative career

    interests about 40 percent of Dalhousie University faculty, 111

alternative personnel policies, 106

applying career development models to faculty, 65–68

Ashby's Law of Requisite Variety, 74

assertive participative governance results in high morale, 73–74

associate or full professors more likely to seek out opportunities for retraining and respecialization, 65

autonomy

    and independence highly valued among senior faculty, 55

    important characteristic of the productive researcher, 69

Axelrod, Joseph

    provided case study of Stephen Abbott, xii

B

Baldwin, R.G.

    does not speculate on how gender differences might play out with regard to faculty careers, 122

    faculty have periods of stability and stressful change, 66

    highest level of career satisfaction is at the final stage, 66

Behnke, Barbara

    coordinator of this work, xi

Bergman, Dean

    assigned weekly sessions at Counseling Center, 14

Boice's study (1993) as a source on how to prevent stuckness, 88

Braskamp and colleagues' application of Levinson's model, 44, 46

"burnout" of faculty is not a significant problem, 9

C

California State university system

    will be in the middle of major face-lifts, 1

camaraderie as a summary of what need, 104–5

campus community

    lack of sense of, 22

career advancement

    senior faculty members have no place to go with regard to, 10

career alternatives, 111–13

    no reason to believe would cost a university its best people, 112

career blocks identification, 87

career development, 60–62

    misapplication of theory to faculty, 68–69

    models based on adult development models, 64–65

    theorists focus too much attention on financial and job-related issues without considering other aspects, 68

career final stage as

    disengagement from commitment and investment in other areas, 63

career-planning activities need, 94

career-related behavior affected by the demands of life cycle, 63

Carl Rogers Counseling Center, 14

cognitive competencies sets

    that must be acquired in a sequential manner, 40

cognitive maturation

    model of adult development that relies on, 43–44

college teachers have unusual opportunities for subcareers, 79

communication
> and distance between faculty correlation, 75–76
> essential to productivity, 74–75

community college faculty primary source of satisfaction
  not autonomy but connectedness, 55–56

complexity of careers greater for women than men, 122

comprehensive
> approach to faculty vitality, 95–102
> needs that must be addressed, 95
> model for development of human and organizational
>> resources, 98
> plan for human and organizational development, 97

conducive institutional environments have decentralized organizations, 74

considerate behaviors as related to effectiveness, 81

content knowledge and skills currency, 52

Corcoran and Clark (1985) study of faculty, 87

Counseling Center of Carl Rogers, 14

critical events. *See* crucial events.

cross-sectional studies problems, 119–21

crucial events
> early in career major causal action, 88
> that significantly influenced careers of faculty, 91–92

culture conflict
> managerial versus faculty, 72

D

Dalhousie University in Canada, 111–12

decentralized organizations
> have conducive institutional environments, 74

department head
> twenty-eight roles for, 116

developmental
> crises, 41
> efforts typically initiated in uncoordinated fashion, 100
> failures make subsequent success more difficult, 41
> sample of activities for approach, 99–100
> strategies, four themes to remember in selection of, 83

Dewey, John
> influence on Abbot of conversations on, 14

discussion of goals, 102

distinctive organizational culture
> has connection with highest employee morale, 70

diversity as a positive feature

so long as the group has the same primary goals and culture, 77

dual identities of women, 46

dual responsibilities of individual and institution interplay, 83–85

E

"early career" in three-stage model, 67–68

early retirement, 109–11

as a stopgap, 111

as a way of losing the best senior faculty and retention of those who should move on, 110–11

effective leadership essential for a vital organization, 80–82

effectiveness

concepts relating to leaders, 81

negative association with rigid decision making, 73–74

employment retention rate connection with the best profits, 56–57

environment of the institution affects quality of

work, attention and service, and own sense of self of faculty, 91

Erikson, Erik

eight stages of life of, 40

Eriksonian developmental stages, 41

Eriksonian model, 40–41

developmental failures carried forward in life making subsequent success more difficult, 41

emphasis on progression through certain life phases can become self-fulfilling if viewed uncritically, 48

essential to productivity

communication as, 74–75

F

factors

in maintaining positive characteristics in senior faculty, 58

that affect vitality of all faculty, 28

faculty. *See also* senior faculty.

"burnout" not a significant problem, 9

career

can be understood in terms of adult development theory, 65

development stages, 45

pattern assumptions may not be accurate, 122

demographics shifting, 6–9

development

attempts usually neither comprehensive nor coordinated, 96

individual-level strategies most often discussed, 85

institutional program descriptions, 95

institution-level strategies least frequently mentioned, 85

program is best when proactive and preventive, 89

programs not seen as facilitating continued vitality, 84

differences as more related to career stage than gender, 122

interviews analysis, 44, 46

joining in late 1960s and early 1970s overwhelmed established professoriat in both numbers and enthusiasm, 107

joining two-year community colleges during the late 1960s and early 1970s often were college founders, 107

morale, 103–4

move through periods of relative stability and of stressful change and transition, 66

obsolescence, research does not support validity of, 9

research productivity measured by using histories of science entries, 31–32

vitality

can't maintain without features of a vital institution, 83

comprehensive approach to, 94–102

institutions can't afford to take a laissez-faire approach, 26

need for specific people to monitor, 94–95

work very social, depending on interactions in environment, 60

Failure to consider individual differences

problems associated with, 121–23

features

affecting senior faculty productivity lack clear profile, 117

facilitating productivity, 81

shared by productive research organizations, 60

that facilitate faculty vitality don't all apply to all, 84

Federal Grant University, 14

Fife, Jonathan

encouragement by, xii

flaws in productivity studies of senior faculty, 34

four-stage model of faculty career development, 66

Freedman (1979)

construct potentially fraught with normative problems, 48

fifth and final stage, 47

used Loevinger's model in description of faculty development, 47

freedom frightening

for those who lived for many years with career constraints, 26
Free Speech Movement at Berkeley effect on teaching, 16
Frost, Libby
prepared figures and tables, xi–xii
functional development approach, 97–98
Furniss three-stage model, 67–68

G

general development strategies, 106
Gennep, Arnold van, 40
Gilligan (1982)
focused differences between men and women in movement through life cycle, 43
"higher" stages of cognitive development are not necessarily
better or universal, 44
goal of more evenly distributing faculty ages, 111
goals that are clear and coordinating, 69–70
good leaders, 80–81
Greene, Elizabeth
provided editing, word processing, and reference management, xi

H

Havighurst (1964)
failures of theory, 64–65
six-stage theory of vocational development, 64
higher education institutions rarely invest heavily in maintaining
the productivity of their faculty, 117
Higher Education Research Institute 1989 results on senior faculty
participation in development programs, 92
highest level of satisfaction with career found at final stage, 66
high-level producers more productive than the remaining two-
thirds had been at their peak, 32–33
"highly active" faculty heavily involved with major decisions on
campus as well as outside the institutions, 55
Hilberry, Conrad
importance of opportunities throughout one's career, 78–79
"hired hands"
managerial culture that treats the faculty like, 72
histories of science entries as criterion of successful contribution to
the body of knowledge, 31
Hodgkinson (1974)

first to apply adult development theory to understanding
the stages of development among faculty, 44
Holland (1985) model and theory of vocational preferences, 62–63
House Un-American Activities Committee
demonstration against, 15
human resources
account for the greatest variance in research productivity, 75
"Hutchins College," 13

I

impact of the institution and its priorities on the faculty member
rarely discussed, 120
importance of opportunities throughout one's career, 78–79
Improving Teaching Styles, 13
inability to lay off faculty
not a barrier to an institution's financial stability, 8–9
independent career development models, 62–64
initiating structure as related to effectiveness, 81
In Our Fifties: Voices of Men and Women Reinventing Their Lives, xi
Institute of Scientific Information sources, 114
institutional
climate, 104–5
culture significance, 70–72
features as powerful predictors of research productivity, 59
leadership by faculty, 106–7
offices disconnected or irrelevant to some faculty members, 106
office to address weak features that affect vitality, 105–6
senior faculty leaders' difference between those from recently
established colleges and those founded many years
ago, 122
institution can't remain productive without creative faculty, 84
integration
senior faculty focus toward, 27
internal factors affecting productivity of senior faculty, 39–58
interplay between the individual and the institution and their
dual responsibilities, 83–85

J

job security of less importance for senior faculty, 10
Johnson, Ross
searched for relevant works, xii
Jung, Carl, 40

K

Kanter, Rosabeth Moss, 78

Kegan (1982) six-stage theory of development, 43

Kelly (1991)

does not identify gender differences among senior faculty, 122

Kerr, Clark

use of term Federal Grant University, 14

key to success as ability to adjust one's sense of self in response to the various experiences one has in specific occupations, 63

knowledge of individual differences among senior faculty may not be accurate, 122

L

lack of clarity regarding differences between stages of development after age 50, 46–47

late career in three-stage model, 68

Law of Requisite Variety, 74

leader role in variance among groups' productivity, 80

leadership training

for senior faculty importance, 81–82

to maintain senior faculty members' vitality, 89

leaders of productive groups consistently seen as excellent, productive scientists, 80

leaves of absence use, 113

Levinson, D.J.

focused on points of transition in Eriksonian model, 43

model as the basis of a three-stage model of faculty careers, 67

model of mature male development, 47

model used to identify faculty members' seven-stage career, 44

study of life cycle, 41

survey of faculty and adult development models borrows from, 46

Lilly fellows survey, 53

linking faculty evaluation and development, 113–14

Loevinger focuses on extent to which one is able to reason and make decisions independent of other people, 44

longitudinal studies lack, 120–21

M

MADFs. *See* middle-aged and disillusioned.

male development model of Levinson
    popular in understanding shifting career needs of faculty, 66
managerial culture that treats the faculty like "hired hands," 72
managerial versus faculty culture conflict, 72
managers must resist centralizing decisions in times of stress, 74
mature level of development success, 48
"Me Generation" student, 19
Men and Women of the Corporation (1977), 78
mental abilities until at least the 60s are constant over time, 28
mentoring colleagues, 108–9
midcareer
    adults have confronted their dreams for a career, 66–67
    faculty find it increasingly difficult to tolerate "endless
        committees and paperwork," 104
    in three-stage model, 68
middle-aged and disillusioned faculty interviews, 88
"midlife" crisis, 43
Minneapolis Star-Tribune letter on institutional attempts
    to incorporate various theories, 71
model of mature male development of Levinson's, 47
models of adult development
    biases, 48
    questionable universality, 49
money as a reward for faculty, 78
monitoring features that facilitate productivity, 101
morale as a desired quality for faculty, 57–58
most productive researchers lose interest in the absence of
    research-oriented colleagues, 76
motivation as personal desire plays a pivotal role in productivity,
    50–52
moving away from former activities
    senior faculty focus toward, 27
multiple-career
    emerging concept supported and documented by Super,
        63–64
    models in understanding faculty revitalization, 65

N

National Center for Education Statistics does not indicate relation-
    ships among various factors, 122
National Education Data Resource Center in Alexandria, Virginia, xii
negative association between
    effectiveness and bureaucratic rigid decision making, 73–74

---

faculty age and teaching if it exists is small, 31

nontraditional faculty members more likely to view prospects of leaving academe as not profoundly upsetting, 61

nontraditional topics for term papers, 18

O

obsolescence
> almost inevitable without efforts to counteract it, 101, 114–15
>
> decreasing resources to prevent, 115
>
> prevention gone from individual to organization's problem, 115

office space correlation between communication and distance between faculty, 75–76

opportunities' importance throughout one's career, 78–79

organizational development approach, 97–98

orientation in early studies
> prolific researchers externally oriented, 55

Ortega y Gasset, Jose, 40

P

"Pacific Rim," 16

performance low when no coordination exists, 69

personal development approach, 97–98
> very little has been done in area of, 96

Piagetian model
> adult development, 43–44
>
> four sets of cognitive competencies that must be acquired in a sequential manner, 40
>
> unsuccessful development results in being stuck at a specific stage of life, 41

place of employment as single best predictor of faculty scholarly productivity, 59

"populist" perspective
> increased access at the expense of quality, 5

positive climate
> correlates positively with productivity, 80
>
> productivity and creativity influenced by, 72–73

"postmodernism," 23

post-tenure review should be structured as part of a faculty professional development program, 113

prevention as best strategy for ensuring ongoing competence of senior faculty, 52 primary personality traits, 62

primary source of satisfaction was not autonomy but connectedness among community college faculty, 55–56

proactive arrangement of opportunities for development, 114

productive

    academic organization components, 40

    institutions rely on the presence of multiple features that singularly are quite fragile, 105

    research organizations share a consistent set of features, 60

productivity

    and creativity influenced by positive climate, 72–73

    balancing coordination and autonomy, 69

    correlates positively with positive group climate, 80

    increases with size of the research group, 76

    of senior faculty

        institutional factors affecting the, 59–82

        internal factors affecting, 39–58

        senior faculty studies flaws, 34–35

    tends to peak around age 40, 32

professional development programs

    no one will appeal to all faculty members, 93

professional meetings away from campus attendance, 92–93

pursuer of knowledge rather than master of it

    shift of Abbot to, 18

Q

quality graduate students and staff positively associated with productivity in research, 76

quality in research more important than quantity for mature faculty members, 35

quality without access is no longer quality, 6

R

Rabbit Angstrom books of John Updike, 13

racial and ethnic minority faculty query on to what extent they are likely to move more slowly up the ranks, 122

rationale of college as a place to earn more money, 20

ratio of high-quality to low-quality publications remains relatively constant over the professional life span, 33

"real" economy achievement, 111

recognition and praise as most highly rated rewards for productivity in research, 78

"reconceptualized" model of career development, 65

relevance

    time when one asks questions about, 27

Renner (1986)

    several concerns of a career alternative policy, 111–12

research productivity

    human resources account for the greatest variance in, 75

"research star" hiring

    lack of success in this strategy to bring up group research productivity, 59

research university mentors as often inappropriate model, 109

resources, 75–76

retention rate significance

    companies earned the best profits with highest employment, 56

retrospective reporting problems, 121

"reverse discrimination," 23

rewards

    faculty are significantly motivated by, 77–78

"right" teaching style doesn't matter so long as instructors and their students are sincere, 24

Rorty, Richard, 23

S

salaries and benefits

    questions that tend to cluster at the higher end, 8

    satisfaction greater in two- as opposed to four-year schools, 77

San Francisco State

    arrival of Abbot to teaching post at, 14

Sax, Greg

    searched for relevant works, xi–xii

scientific expertise of the leader best predicted a group's productivity, 80

senior faculty, 3. *See also* faculty.

    beneficiaries of the least amount of professional development services when they appreciate them most, 92

    "burnout" not apparent, 57–58

    erroneous knowledge of individual differences among, 122

    interpretation enhanced by many years of study of field, 36

    largest faculty cohort in American higher education history, 107

    more likely to solve problems independently, 104

    most interesting and capable people, 118

college teachers have unusual opportunities for, 79
successful academic careers
    four factors that support, 77
Super's model, 63–64

T

teaching
    effectiveness age negatively related to, 29, 30
    role socialization less important when today's senior faculty
        were hired, 108–9
    senior faculty commit about the same amount of time as
        younger faculty to, 29
theory of expectancy, 51–52
The University Teacher as Artist, 13
three-stage model
    not related to age, 68
    of faculty careers, 67
together for a longer length of time positively associated with
   quantity and quality of research, 77
top-priority goals emphasis, 70
traditional approaches to faculty vitality, 91–94
traditional faculty, 60–62
    likely to view career shifting as daunting, 61
trapped in their academic professions, certain faculty more likely to
   feel this than others, 122

U

university goals change from education to training, 19–20
University of California will be in the middle of major face-lifts, 1
University of Chicago under Hutchins, 13
University of Minnesota
    Corcoran and Clark (1985) study of faculty at, 87
    thanking staff for support, xi
    will have revised its structure and commitment, 1
unsuccessful development results in being stuck at a specific stage
   of life, 41
Updike, John
    books on Rabbit Angstrom, 13
U.S. National Center for Education Statistics, help, xii

V

variation in type of data-retrieval system in discipline as flaw in
   productivity studies of senior faculty, 34

vital

W

Y

ASHE-ERIC HIGHER EDUCATION REPORTS

Since 1983, the Association for the Study of Higher Education (ASHE) and the Educational Resources Information Center (ERIC) Clearinghouse on Higher Education, a sponsored project of the Graduate School of Education and Human Development at The George Washington University, have cosponsored the ASHE-ERIC Higher Education Report series. This volume is the twenty-fifth overall and the eighth to be published by the Graduate School of Education and Human Development at The George Washington University.

Each monograph is the definitive analysis of a tough higher education problem, based on thorough research of pertinent literature and institutional experiences. Topics are identified by a national survey. Noted practitioners and scholars are then commissioned to write the reports, with experts providing critical reviews of each manuscript before publication.

Eight monographs (10 before 1985) in the ASHE-ERIC Higher Education Report series are published each year and are available on individual and subscription bases. To order, use the order form on the last page of this book.

Qualified persons interested in writing a monograph for the ASHE-ERIC Higher Education Report series are invited to submit a proposal to the National Advisory Board. As the preeminent literature review and issue analysis series in higher education, the Higher Education Reports are guaranteed wide dissemination and national exposure for accepted candidates. Execution of a monograph requires at least a minimal familiarity with the ERIC database, including *Resources in Education* and the current *Index to Journals in Education*. The objective of these reports is to bridge conventional wisdom with practical research. Prospective authors are strongly encouraged to call Dr. Fife at (800) 773-3742.

For further information, write to
ASHE-ERIC Higher Education Reports
The George Washington University
One Dupont Circle, Suite 630
Washington, DC 20036
Or phone (202) 296-2597; toll free: (800) 773-ERIC.

Write or call for a complete catalog.

Visit our Web site at **www.gwu.edu/~eriche**

ADVISORY BOARD

James Earl Davis
University of Delaware at Newark

Kenneth A. Feldman
SUNY at Stoney Brook

Cassie Freeman
Peabody College, Vanderbilt University

Susan Frost
Emory University

Mildred Garcia
Arizona State University West

Philo Hutcheson
Georgia State University

CONSULTING EDITORS

Sandra Beyer
University of Texas at El Paso

Robert Boice
State University of New York–Stony Brook

Steve Brigham
American Association for Higher Education

Ivy E. Broder
The American University

Nevin C. Brown
The Education Trust, Inc.

Shirley M. Clark
Oregon State System of Higher Education

Robert A. Cornesky
Cornesky and Associates, Inc.

Cheryl Falk
Yakima Valley Community College

Anne H. Frank
American Association of University Professors

Michelle D. Gilliard
Consortium for the Advancement of Private Higher
  Education–The Council of Independent Colleges

Joseph E. Gilmore
Northwest Missouri State University

Arthur Greenberg
Community School District 25, Flushing, New York

Dean L. Hubbard
Northwest Missouri State University

Edward Johnson
Arizona Commission for Post Seconday Education

Clara M. Lovett
Northern Arizona University

Laurence R. Marcus
Rowan College

Robert Menges
Northwestern University

Diane E. Morrison
Centre for Curriculum, Trensfer and Technology

L. Jackson Newell
University of Utah

Steven G. Olswang
University of Washington

Laura W. Perna
Frederick D. Patterson Research
  Institute of the College Fund/UNCF

R. Eugene Rice
American Association for Higher Education

Brent Ruben
State University of New Jersey–Rutgers

Sherry Sayles-Folks
Eastern Michigan University

Jack H. Schuster
Claremont Graduate School—Center for Educational Studies

Daniel Seymour
Claremont College–California

Marilla D. Svinicki
University of Texas–Austin

David Sweet
OERI, U.S. Department of Education

Gershon Vincow
Syracuse University

Dan W. Wheeler
University of Nebraska—Lincoln

Donald H. Wulff
University of Washington

Manta Yorke
Liverpool John Moores University

REVIEW PANEL

Charles Adams
University of Massachusetts–Amherst

Louis Albert
American Association for Higher Education

Richard Alfred
University of Michigan

Henry Lee Allen
University of Rochester

Philip G. Altbach
Boston College

Marilyn J. Amey
University of Kansas

Kristine L. Anderson
Florida Atlantic University

Karen D. Arnold
Boston College

Robert J. Barak
Iowa State Board of Regents

Alan Bayer
Virginia Polytechnic Institute and State University

John P. Bean
Indiana University–Bloomington

John M. Braxton
Peabody College, Vanderbilt University

Ellen M. Brier
Tennessee State University

Barbara E. Brittingham
The University of Rhode Island

Dennis Brown
University of Kansas

Peter McE. Buchanan
Council for Advancement and Support of Education

Patricia Carter
University of Michigan

John A. Centra
Syracuse University

Arthur W. Chickering
George Mason University

Darrel A. Clowes
Virginia Polytechnic Institute and State University

Cynthia S. Dickens
Mississippi State University

Deborah M. DiCroce
Piedmont Virginia Community College

Sarah M. Dinham
University of Arizona

Kenneth A. Feldman
State University of New York–Stony Brook

Dorothy E. Finnegan
The College of William & Mary

Mildred Garcia
Montclair State College

Rodolfo Z. Garcia
Commission on Institutions of Higher Education

Kenneth C. Green
University of Southern California

James Hearn
University of Georgia

Edward R. Hines
Illinois State University

Deborah Hunter
University of Vermont

Philo Hutcheson
Georgia State University

Bruce Anthony Jones
University of Pittsburgh

Elizabeth A. Jones
The Pennsylvania State University

Kathryn Kretschmer
University of Kansas

Marsha V. Krotseng
State College and University Systems of West Virginia

George D. Kuh
Indiana University–Bloomington

Daniel T. Layzell
University of Wisconsin System

Patrick G. Love
Kent State University

Cheryl D. Lovell
State Higher Education Executive Officers

Meredith Jane Ludwig
American Association of State Colleges and Universities

Dewayne Matthews
Western Interstate Commission for Higher Education

Mantha V. Mehallis
Florida Atlantic University

Toby Milton
Essex Community College

James R. Mingle
State Higher Education Executive Officers

John A. Muffo
Virginia Polytechnic Institute and State University

L. Jackson Newell
Deep Springs College

James C. Palmer
Illinois State University

Robert A. Rhoads
The Pennsylvania State University

G. Jeremiah Ryan
Harford Community College

Mary Ann Danowitz Sagaria
The Ohio State University

Daryl G. Smith
The Claremont Graduate School

William G. Tierney
University of Southern California

Susan B. Twombly
University of Kansas

Robert A. Walhaus
University of Illinois–Chicago

Harold Wechsler
University of Rochester

Elizabeth J. Whitt
University of Illinois–Chicago

Michael J. Worth
The George Washington University

RECENT TITLES

Volume 25 ASHE-ERIC Higher Education Reports

1. A Culture for Academic Excellence: Implementing the Quality Principles in Higher Education
   Jann E. Freed, Marie R. Klugman, and Jonathan D. Fife

2. From Discipline to Development: Rethinking Student Conduct in Higher Education
   Michael Dannells

3. Academic Controversy: Enriching College Instruction through Intellectual Conflict
   David W. Johnson, Roger T. Johnson, and Karl A. Smith

4. Higher Education Leadership: Analyzing the Gender Gap
   Luba Chliwniak

5. The Virtual Campus: Technology and Reform in Higher Education
   Gerald C. Van Dusen

6. Early Intervention Programs: Opening the Door to Higher Education
   Robert H. Fenske, Christine A. Geranios, Jonathan E. Keller, and David E. Moore

Volume 24 ASHE-ERIC Higher Education Reports

1. Tenure, Promotion, and Reappointment: Legal and Administrative Implications (951)
   Benjamin Baez and John A. Centra

2. Taking Teaching Seriously: Meeting the Challenge of Instructional Improvement (952)
   Michael B. Paulsen and Kenneth A. Feldman

3. Empowering the Faculty: Mentoring Redirected and Renewed (953)
   Gaye Luna and Deborah L. Cullen

4. Enhancing Student Learning: Intellectual, Social, and Emotional Integration (954)
   Anne Goodsell Love and Patrick G. Love

5. Benchmarking in Higher Education: Adapting Best Practices to Improve Quality (955)
   Jeffrey W. Alstete

6. Models for Improving College Teaching: A Faculty Resource (956)
   Jon E. Travis

7. Experiential Learning in Higher Education: Linking Classroom and Community (957)
   Jeffrey A. Cantor

8. Successful Faculty Development and Evaluation: The Complete Teaching Portfolio (958)
   John P. Murray

Volume 23 ASHE-ERIC Higher Education Reports

1. The Advisory Committee Advantage: Creating an Effective Strategy for Programmatic Improvement (941)
   Lee Teitel

2. Collaborative Peer Review: The Role of Faculty in Improving College Teaching (942)
   Larry Keig and Michael D. Waggoner

3. Prices, Productivity, and Investment: Assessing Financial Strategies in Higher Education (943)
   Edward P. St. John

4. The Development Officer in Higher Education: Toward an Understanding of the Role (944)
   Michael J. Worth and James W. Asp II

5. Measuring Up: The Promises and Pitfalls of Performance Indicators in Higher Education (945)
   Gerald Gaither, Brian P. Nedwek, and John E. Neal

6. A New Alliance: Continuous Quality and Classroom Effectiveness (946)
   Mimi Wolverton

7. Redesigning Higher Education: Producing Dramatic Gains in Student Learning (947)
   Lion F. Gardiner

8. Student Learning outside the Classroom: Transcending Artificial Boundaries (948)
   George D. Kuh, Katie Branch Douglas, Jon P. Lund, and Jackie Ramin-Gyurnek

Volume 22 ASHE-ERIC Higher Education Reports

1. The Department Chair: New Roles, Responsibilities, and Challenges (931)
   Alan T. Seagren, John W. Creswell, and Daniel W. Wheeler

2. Sexual Harassment in Higher Education: From Conflict to Community (932)
   Robert O. Riggs, Patricia H. Murrell, and JoAnne C. Cutting

3. Chicanos in Higher Education: Issues and Dilemmas for the 21st Century (933)
   Adalberto Aguirre Jr., and Ruben O. Martinez

4. Academic Freedom in American Higher Education: Rights, Responsibilities, and Limitations (934)
   Robert K. Poch

ORDER FORM

Quantity   **Amount**

_____ Please begin my subscription to the current year's *ASHE-ERIC Higher Education Reports* (Volume 25) at $120.00, over 33% off the cover price, starting with Report 1.   _____

_____ Please send a complete set of Volume ____ *ASHE-ERIC Higher Education Reports* at $120.00, over 33% off the cover price.   _____

Individual reports are available for $24.00 and include the cost of shipping and handling.

SHIPPING POLICY:
- Books are sent UPS Ground or equivalent. For faster delivery, call for charges.
- Alaska, Hawaii, U.S. Territories, and Foreign Countries, please call for shipping information.
- Order will be shipped within 24 hours after receipt of request.
- Orders of 10 or more books, call for shipping information.

All prices shown are subject to change.

Returns: No cash refunds—credit will be applied to future orders.

PLEASE SEND ME THE FOLLOWING REPORTS:

Quantity	Volume/No.	Title	Amount

Please check one of the following:
- ☐ Check enclosed, payable to GW-ERIC.
- ☐ Purchase order attached.
- ☐ Charge my credit card indicated below:
  - ☐ Visa   ☐ MasterCard

Subtotal: _____
Less Discount: _____
Total Due: _____

Expiration Date_____

Name_____

Title_____

Institution _____

Address_____

City _____ State _____ Zip_____

Phone _____ Fax _____Telex_____

Signature _____ Date_____

SEND ALL ORDERS TO: ASHE-ERIC Higher Education Reports
The George Washington University
One Dupont Cir., Ste. 630, Washington, DC 20036-1183
Phone: (202) 296-2597 • Toll-free: (800) 773-ERIC
FAX: (202) 452-1844
URL: www.gwu.edu/~eriche

DATE DUE